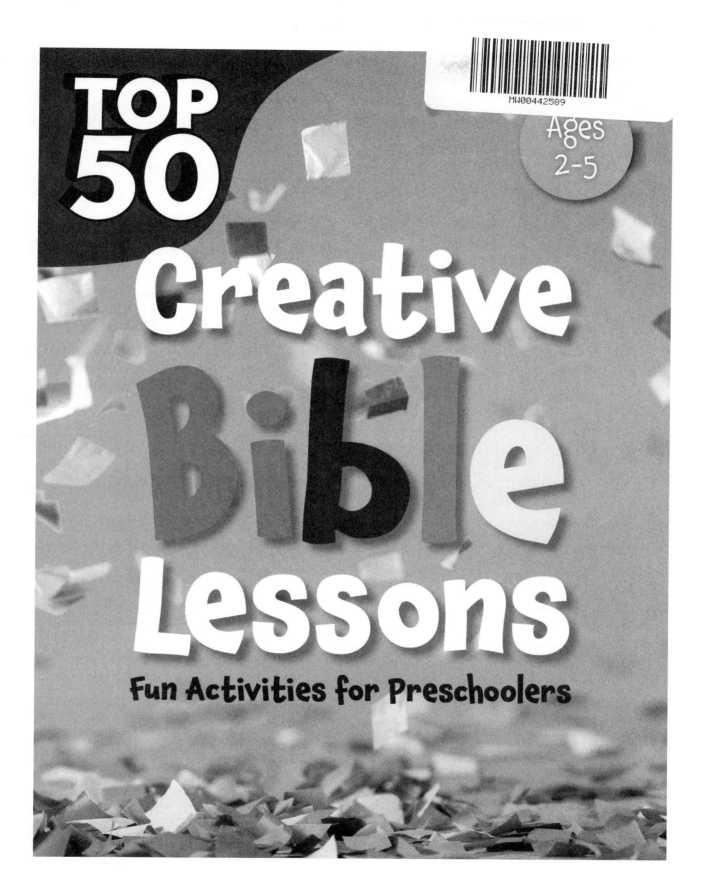

TOP 50

Ages 2-5

Creative Bible Lessons

Fun Activities for Preschoolers

 HENDRICKSON PUBLISHERS ROSE KiDZ

Top 50 Creative Bible Lessons: Fun Activities for Preschoolers

© 2019 Rose Publishing, LLC.

RoseKidz® is an imprint of
Rose Publishing, LLC
P.O. Box 3473
Peabody, Massachusetts 01961-3473 USA
www.hendricksonrose.com/rosekidz

Managing Editor: Karen McGraw
Editorial and Production Associate: Drew McCall
Assistant Editor: Talia Messina

Cover Design: Drew McCall
Interior Typography: Karen McGraw

Conditions of Use

Unless otherwise indicated, all Scripture quotations are taken from the Holy Bible, New Living Translation, copyright © 1996, 2004, 2015 by Tyndale House Foundation. Used by permission of Tyndale House Publishers, Inc., Carol Stream, Illinois 60188. All rights reserved.

ISBN: 978-1-58411-156-6
RoseKidz® reorder# R38255
RELIGION/Christian Ministry/Children

Printed in United States of America
Printed December 2019

Table of Contents

Introduction

Super-Sized Fun for Preschoolers

There is nothing like seeing the happy face of a young child—especially when the child is engaged in learning Bible stories while enjoying fun activities. That's where *Top 50 Creative Bible Lessons* comes in. It's jammed full of exciting Bible stories and creative activities sure to keep young minds learning.

It's Easy to Use

Top 50 Creative Bible Lessons includes classic Bible stories, each followed by a set of related activities for children two to five years old. The story pages include a memory verse, a Bible story, and a few suggested discussion questions to help kids further understand the story's lesson.

After reading a Bible story with the children and talking about it, parents or leaders guide the kids through the activities relating to the story.

- Each activity page includes a **What you need** list of materials. Most items needed for the activities are simple craft or school supplies, and many are commonly found around the house.

- Easy step-by-step **What to do** instructions guide you through each activity.

- Many pages in the book are reproducible. It's okay to copy these reproducible pages so that you can cut out the patterns and images for a single child or for a group of children.

- Each lesson also includes a **Take-Home Page** to continue the learning at home.

Interactive Fun!

Top 50 Creative Bible Lessons is a huge book of interactive fun! Parents or teachers can set up each project for the children based on the simple instructions, and then guide them through the activity. For activities such as mazes, color codes, connect-the-dots, picture puzzles, and picture searches, adults may read the instructions aloud and let the kids work on their own.

Most of the activities include adult involvement. The many arts and crafts projects, and snack activities, for instance, allow an opportunity for caring adults to interact with the children.

Top 50 Creative Bible Lessons is also perfect for play-dates or busy classrooms. All the activities in this book are designed so that groups of kids can participate in each project.

On the other hand, most of the activities can be shared with an individual child. Parents can easily spend quality one-on-one time with their child using these enjoyable projects.

Variety is the key! Don't worry about kids getting bored; there are hundreds of activities to choose from.

God Makes Everything

memory verse

The LORD God made all. Genesis 2:9

Creation of Heaven and Earth (based on Genesis 1—2)

God made everything in the world. At first, there was nothing.

On the first day, God said, "Let there light," and there was light. God made the first day and night.

On the second day, God separated the water from the land to make sky, land, and seas.

On the third day, God made all the growing plants and trees.

On the fourth day, God made the sun and moon, and he made the stars and set them all in the sky.

On the fifth day, God made fish for the seas and birds for the sky.

On the sixth day, God made every living creature. Then, he created man and woman.

Each time God created something new, he said, "It is good." God loves the world he made. God loves the people he created, too.

God had a wonderful plan to make a world.

 ## discussion questions

1. Who made the world?

2. What did God say when he created each thing?

Night-Time Sky

What you need

- scissors or papercutter
- black construction paper
- glue

What you do

1. For each child, photocopy this page. Cut out the stars and moon for each child. Older children may be able to cut for themselves. Lay a sheet of black construction paper on the table for each child.
2. Put a spot of glue on each paper. Then, have the child place the moon in the "sky."
3. Put five more spots of glue on the page and let the child place stars in the sky.

What to Say

God made the skies. During the day, the skies are bright and sunny. At night, the skies look black. But God put something beautiful in the night sky for us to see.

Creation Puppets

What you need

- scissors or papercutter
- paper-towel tubes
- tape
- crayons or markers

What you do

1. Photocopy this page, making enough copies for each child to choose one animal. Cut out animal figures. Older children may be able to cut for themselves.

2. Have the children color their chosen creation figure.

3. Help them tape the figure to the top part of a paper-towel tube.

4. Have the children hold up their puppets. Encourage them to name the creature they are holding.

Who made the fish? Who made the bird? Who made the elephant?

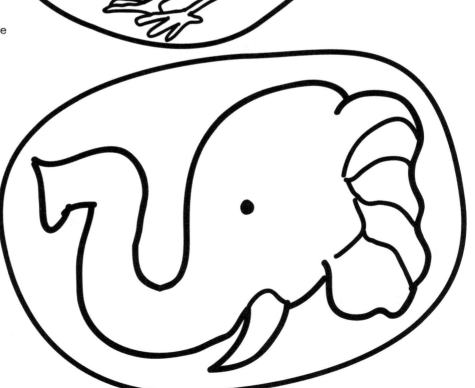

A Garden Home

What you need

- scissors or papercutter
- crayons or markers
- glue

What you do

1. For each child, photocopy this page. Cut out the picture and Adam and Eve figures. Older children may be able to cut for themselves.

2. Say, **Adam and Eve were the first people God made. God also made them a beautiful garden where they could live.**

3. Children color the pictures. Then, they glue Adam and Eve to the picture of the garden.

God Makes Everything

Creation of Heaven and Earth (based on Genesis 1—2)

memory verse

The LORD God made all. Genesis 2:9

discussion questions

1. Who made the world?

2. What did God say when he created each thing?

The First Family

Adam and Eve and their sons were the first family. God gives us families because he loves us. Each family member has a special job. Look at this picture. Can you tell what each person's job was? Cain was a farmer. Abel took care of the sheep. Adam fished and Eve sewed.

Hidden in this picture are tools that each person needs. Can you find them? There is a spear, a shepherd's staff, a garden hoe, and some thread and a needle. Draw a line to the person who will use each tool.

Noah Obeys

memory verse

Noah did everything exactly as God had commanded him. Genesis 6:22

The Big Boat (based on Genesis 6—9)

God told Noah to build a big boat. The boat was called an *ark*. Noah did just as God told him. He built the ark.

God then told Noah to take his family and two of every kind of animal into the ark to protect them from a great flood. God wanted to be sure the animals and Noah's family were safe.

Noah obeyed God. All during the flood, God took care of Noah, his family, and all the animals. God takes care of us, too.

When the flood was over, God told Noah to send a dove out of the ark. Noah obeyed. When the dove came back carrying an olive branch, Noah knew it was safe to come out of the ark.

Noah, his family, and all the animals came out of the ark. Obeying God made Noah happy. He built an altar to God. He thanked God and praised him.

God sent a beautiful rainbow. The rainbow was God's promise never to flood the earth again. God keeps his promises to us. Every time we see a rainbow, we can remember God's promise to take care of us.

? discussion questions

1. What was Noah's boat called?
2. How many of each animal did Noah put on the ark?
3. What did God put in the sky to help us remember his promise?

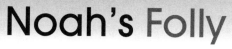

Noah's Folly

What you need

- scissors or papercutter
- crayons or markers

What you do

1. For each child, photocopy this page and cut out the activity. Older children may be able to cut for themselves.

2. Children complete the dot-to-dot and then color in the picture.

What to Say

Noah was 600 years old when he went into the ark! People lived a long time when God first made the world. When Noah was building the ark, everyone laughed at him. His friends, neighbors, and maybe even some family members thought he was a little crazy. But when it started to rain and didn't stop, they didn't think he was so crazy!

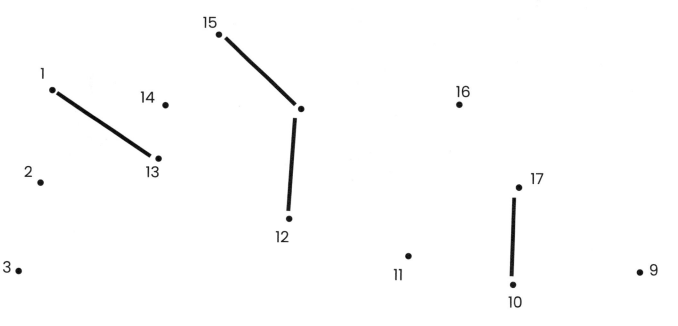

Hard Work

What you need

- scissors or papercutter
- crayons or markers

What you do

1. For each child, photocopy this page and cut out the matching activity.

2. Say, **There was a lot of work to be done in the ark. The animals had to be fed and watered. Food had to be prepared for the meals. The animals' pens had to be kept cleaned and filled with fresh straw. Noah and his family worked hard on the ark. Some of these things might have been used by Noah's family on the ark. Some of these things we use today.**

3. Children color pictures and draw a line from the Bible-times item to the matching item we use today.

Two of Each Kind

What you need

- scissors or papercutter
- crayons or markers

What you do

1. For each child, photocopy this page and cut out the comparison activity.
Older children may be able to cut for themselves.

2. Color the pictures in each row that look the same as the first picture in that row.

What to Say

Noah obeyed God. How many of each animal did God tell Noah to take on the boat? Can you find the turtles that are like the first ones? What kind of bird did Noah send out of the boat? What did God put in the sky? We can obey God like Noah did!

Noah Obeys

The Big Boat (based on Genesis 6—9)

memory verse

Noah did everything exactly as God had commanded him. Genesis 6:22

discussion questions

1. What was Noah's boat called?

2. How many of each animal did Noah put on the ark?

3. What did God put in the sky to help us remember his promise?

The Dove Returns

Noah obeyed God and stayed in the ark until God said it was time to come out. We should obey God, too, and live as he says.

Help the dove find its way back to the ark. Follow the maze with your finger or a crayon.

God's Promise to Abraham

memory verse

I trust in [God's] word. Psalm 119:42

As Numerous as the Stars (based on Genesis 12:1–8, 15:3–6, 21:1–5)

The Bible tells us that a man named Abraham loved God very much. One day God spoke to him. "Abraham, I want you and your family to move. I will show you where I want you to live."

Abraham trusted God. He packed up his family, and they started the long journey. God was pleased. One day, as they were traveling, God made a promise to Abraham. "I will make your people a great people, Abraham. I will bless you and make your name great. Everyone here on earth will be blessed because of you."

What a promise! On the way, they stopped at a place called Moreh. Again, God spoke to Abraham: "Abraham, I will give all this land to your children." In honor of God's promise, Abraham made an altar and worshiped God.

Abraham wondered how this land could belong to his children when he did not have any children. He was old, and his wife, Sarah, was old.

Abraham and his family finally came to Canaan, the land where God wanted them to live. Again, God spoke to Abraham: "Look up, Abraham. See all the stars in the sky?"

Abraham looked at the twinkling stars in sky. "Yes, Lord, there are many, many stars."

"You will have many in your family," promised God. "You will have children, your children will have children, and those children will have children. You will have more descendants than the stars in the sky. This land, Canaan, will belong to them."

Another big promise! But Abraham knew God always keeps the promises he makes. When Abraham was 100 years old, Sarah gave birth to a son. Abraham named his son Isaac, just as God told him to.

discussion questions

1. What did God ask Abraham and his family to do?
2. What did God promise to give Abraham?

A New Home

What you need

- scissors or papercutter
- crayons or markers

What you do

1. For each child, photocopy this page and cut out the letters and picture.
   Older children may be able to cut for themselves.
2. Children color the picture.
3. Older children cross out the lower-case letters at the bottom of the page.
   Children write the remaining letters on the blank lines.

What to Say

The letters you wrote spell the name of where Abraham went. Abraham left his home and traveled to Canaan because he trusted God would keep his promises.

wCrtAqNpzAgiAkN _ _ _ _ _ _

Promise Star

What you need

- scissors
- white or other light-colored card stock
- glow-in-the-dark star stickers

What you do

1. For each child, photocopy this page onto card stock. For younger children, cut out the stars and cut on dashed line. Older children may be able to cut for themselves.
2. Children put stars together by sliding one inside the other using the slots you cut. Stars should be able to stand up.
3. Children place glow-in-the-dark star stickers on their stand-up stars.

For Older Children: Older children may be able to cut stars out on their own.

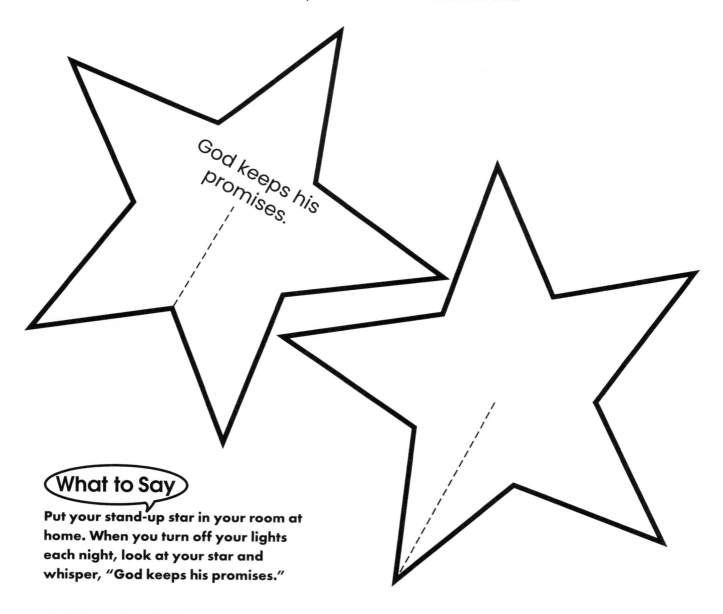

God keeps his promises.

What to Say

Put your stand-up star in your room at home. When you turn off your lights each night, look at your star and whisper, "God keeps his promises."

Night-Time Poster

What you need

- scissors or papercutter
- hole punch
- black construction paper
- yarn
- star stickers
- glue
- yellow crayons or markers

What you do

1. Photocopy a moon and verse paper for each child, and then cut each one out. Older children may be able to cut for themselves.
2. Punch two holes at the top of each sheet of construction paper, and tie yarn through the holes to create a hanger.
3. Children color the moons, and then glue the moons in the center of their black papers.
4. Children place star stickers around their moons.
5. Children glue the verse to the bottom center of the posters.

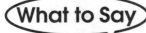

What to Say

Hang your poster in your room to remind you that God always keeps his promises.

> *Starry, starry light*
> *Starry stars so bright*
> *Remind me of God's promises,*
> *Every day and night.*
>
> "I trust in [God's] word." Psalm 119:42

God's Promise to Abraham

As Numerous as the Stars (based on Genesis 12:1–8, 15:3–6, 21:1–5)

 memory verse

I trust in [God's] word. Psalm 119:42

 discussion questions

1. What did God ask Abraham and his family to do?

2. What did God promise to give Abraham?

Hidden Stars

Find the stars and color them. How many stars can you count?

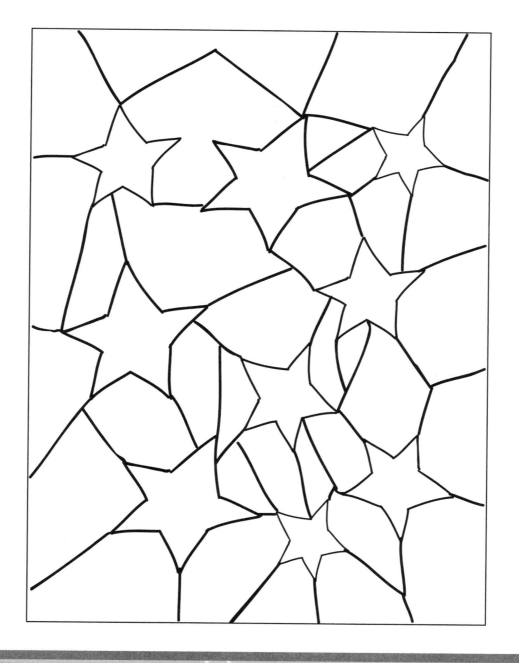

A Wife for Isaac

memory verse

Be kind to each other. Ephesians 4:32

I'll Water Your Camels (based on Genesis 24:1–21)

Abraham thought it was time for his son Isaac to find a wife. He decided to talk to the man he most trusted of all the men who worked for him.

"I want you to go back to the town where I was born," Abraham told his helper. "God will show you the girl he wants Isaac to marry."

So Abraham's helper left for Ur. He piled his camels with gifts to present to the chosen woman.

How am I going to find the right wife for Isaac? the man wondered as he traveled along. *I know she should be a kind girl—and polite.*

Abraham's helper wasn't sure where to look for the right girl, so he prayed for God's help.

"Lord, when I stop at the well," he prayed, "I will ask a girl for water. If she is kind and offers water for my camels, too, I will know she is the one you have chosen for Isaac."

As the man rode up to the well on his camel, he noticed one particularly beautiful girl. Her name was Rebekah.

Rebekah looked up and smiled at Abraham's helper. As the man came down from his camel, he asked Rebekah, "Will you draw me a drink of water?"

Rebekah quickly fetched a drink for him. "Enjoy your drink, sir," she said. Then she drew more water for his camels.

The man's heart began to pound with excitement. This polite girl was the answer to his prayers! She was even kind to the animals!

Abraham's helper was happy when he returned with Rebekah for Isaac. He knew Abraham would be pleased. God had shown him the right wife for Isaac. Rebekah had a kind and loving heart—a heart for God.

discussion questions

1. How was Rebekah kind and courteous to Abraham's servant?
2. How can you be kind and courteous to others?

Camel Jangles

What you need

- white card stock
- scissors or papercutter
- hole punch
- construction paper
- ribbon
- crayons or markers
- glue
- small jingle bells, one for each child

What you do

1. On card stock, photocopy and cut out a camel head for each child. Older children may be able to cut for themselves. Punch holes where indicated.

2. Cut construction paper into 2×8-inch strips and ribbon into 8-inch lengths.

3. Children color their camels.

4. Instruct each child to glue a camel to the center of a paper strip.

5. Assist children in threading ribbons through the holes on the camels and the jingle bells. Tie the ends in a bow.

6. Tape together the ends of the paper strips around the children's wrists.

For Older Children: Before taping strips into wristbands, older children print *Be Kind* on their strips of construction paper.

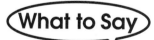 **What to Say**

When you wear your camel jangle, you will be reminded to be kind to others. God is happy when we are kind and not disrespectful.

Kind Words Bingo

What you need

- scissors or papercutter
- glue

What you do

1. Photocopy this page and page 23. Cut out a bingo board, camel set, and happy face markers for each child. Older children may be able to cut at least some of the items for themselves. Enlarge one set of camels to use as game pieces.
2. Children glue their camel squares to their bingo boards in any sequence.
3. Demonstrate to the children how you will hold up a game piece, and they will look to see where their matching camels are. Children cover their matching camels with happy face markers.
4. Repeat, until one or more children get three happy face markers in a row. Children with three markers in a row turn to a child sitting beside them and say something kind.

What to Say

Bingo! What a fun way to practice being kind to others.
We make God happy when we are kind.

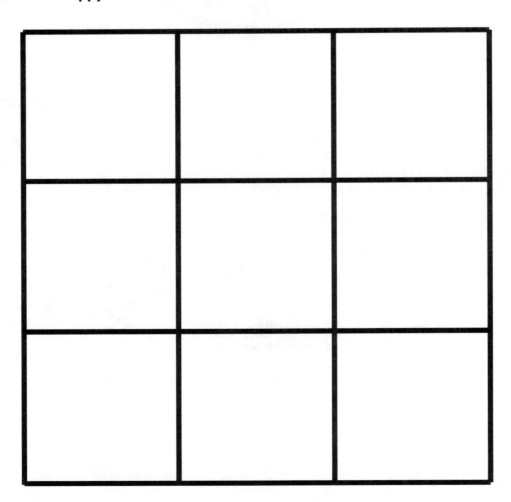

Rebekah Is Kind

What you need

- scissors or papercutter
- crayons or markers

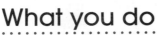

What you do

1. For each child, photocopy this page and cut out matching activity. Older children may be able to cut for themselves.
2. Children draw a line between the jars that are alike.
3. Say, **Rebekah drew water from the well to show kindness to Abraham's helper. Because Rebekah was kind, Abraham's servant knew she was the girl God had chosen for Isaac to marry. God wants us to be kind to others, too.**

A Wife for Isaac

I'll Water Your Camels (based on Genesis 24:1–21)

memory verse
. . . .

Be kind to each other. Ephesians 4:32

discussion questions
. . . .

1. How was Rebekah kind and courteous to Abraham's servant?

2. How can you be kind and courteous to others?

Kindness Puzzle

Draw a picture of a time when someone was kind to you. Cut it into pieces on the lines and put it back together.

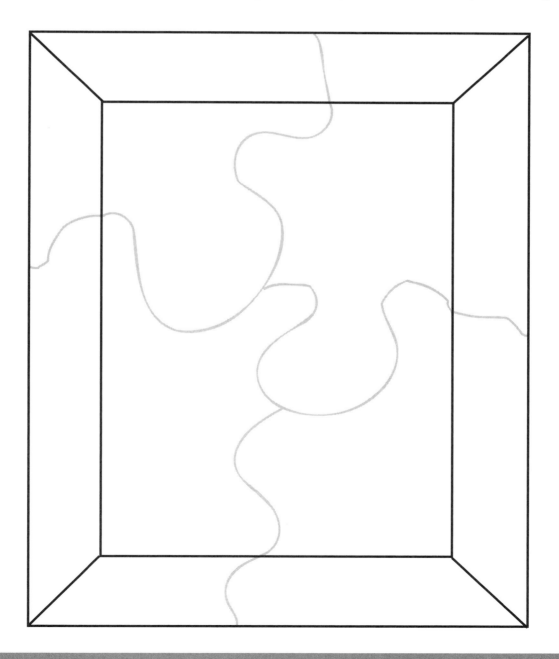

Joseph's Colorful Coat

memory verse

The LORD your God is with you wherever you go. Joshua 1:9

Joseph's Family (based on Genesis 37)

Joseph lived with his father, Jacob, in Canaan. Joseph had ten older brothers and one younger brother. Joseph was Jacob's favorite son. Joseph worked hard for his father. He tended the sheep and took food to his older brothers working in the fields. Joseph was a good boy, and he obeyed his father.

Because Jacob loved Joseph, he made him a colorful coat. Instead of being happy that Joseph had a beautiful new coat, his brothers became angry and jealous.

One morning Joseph told his brothers, "I had a dream last night. We were all tying bundles of grain in the fields. Suddenly, my bundle stood straight up, and your bundles bowed down to it."

When they heard about his dream, Joseph's brothers hated him even more. "We'll never bow down to you," they said.

Joseph was sad his brothers were angry with him. "When will my brothers show kindness to me?" he wondered. But Joseph knew God was in charge. So he trusted that God would take care of him.

Joseph's brothers hated him so much! The brothers argued about what they should do with Joseph. Some of his brothers even wanted to kill him! But Joseph's brother Judah said that was going too far.

Instead, one day, when no one else was around, the brothers took Joseph and threw him into a hole in the ground! When they saw a group of people from Egypt traveling nearby, the brothers sold Joseph to the people as a slave. Joseph was taken far away from his home to Egypt. He had to live in a new country with new people. But Joseph took someone with him—God was with Joseph, even in this strange new place. God was with Joseph everywhere he went! And God is with us, too!

discussion questions

1. What special gift did Joseph's father give him?
2. Why did Joseph's brothers sell him off to be taken to Egypt?

Different Places

What you need

- scissors or papercutter
- crayons or markers

What you do

1. For each child, photocopy this page and cut out activity. Older children may be able to cut for themselves.
2. Children circle the pictures of the places where Joseph went and cross out places Joseph did not go.
3. Children color their pictures of Joseph and his colorful coat.

What to Say

Joseph went to lots of different places! And everywhere he went, God was with him. Joseph didn't go to a playground, but you probably do. When you go to the playground, God is with you! Where are some of the other places you go? God is with you there!

Missing Parts

What you need

- scissors or papercutter
- crayons or markers

What you do

1. For each child, photocopy this page and cut out the drawing activity. Older children may be able to cut for themselves.

2. Children draw in what is missing so that all the pictures in each row match.

What to Say

One picture in each of the rows below is missing. Draw in the missing parts so that they will match the other pictures in the row.

Crafty Camel

What you need

- scissors or papercutter
- construction paper
- fabric scraps
- crayons or markers
- glue

What you do

1. For each child, photocopy this page and cut out the camel, following the dashed and solid lines. Older children may be able to cut for themselves. Cut construction paper into 7-inch squares and fold in half. Cut fabric scraps into 2½-inch squares.
2. Children color the camel and then glue it to a folded construction-paper square so that the camel stands up. You can glue a square of fabric on the camel for a blanket.
3. Say, **When Joseph's brothers sent Joseph far away, he probably rode a camel. God was with Joseph when he was in the country far away, just like God is with you now. The camel can help you remember that God is with you wherever you go.**

Take-Home Paper

Joseph's Many-Colored Coat (based on Genesis 37)

memory verse

The LORD your God is with you wherever you go. Joshua 1:9

discussion questions

1. What special gift did Joseph's father give him?

2. Why did Joseph's brothers sell him off to be taken to Egypt?

Color-Code Coat

Color the sections with ☐s purple.

Color the sections with ◇s orange.

Color the sections with ○s blue.

Joseph in Prison

memory verse

[God] has created us . . . so we can do the good things he planned for us. Ephesians 2:10

Doing Good Work (based on Genesis 37—50)

When Joseph was a boy, his brothers hated him! They took his beautiful coat, a gift from their father, and sold Joseph to traders who were traveling to faraway lands. The traders took Joseph to Egypt, where he became a slave.

One day, the wife of Joseph's master told a terrible lie about Joseph, claiming Joseph had done something wrong. The master believed his wife's lie and had Joseph put in prison.

Even though Joseph did not like being in prison, he asked God to help him be cheerful. Knowing God was with him—even in prison—made Joseph's heart happy.

It didn't take the jailer long to notice how happy Joseph was. He saw how Joseph sang to calm a tired prisoner. He also saw how Joseph gave some of his food to another prisoner who was hungry. The jailer knew Joseph could be trusted.

"Joseph," the jailer said, "I am going to make you head of the prison."

Joseph was happy for the job the jailer gave him. He was responsible and worked hard to take care of the prisoners. Each morning, he took water and cloths to the prisoners so that they could wash up.

When the prisoners asked how he could be so happy, Joseph told them, "My God is with me."

Joseph was faithful to God and worked hard at his job. So God worked through Joseph and gave him the ability to explain people's dreams to them.

When the king of Egypt had a dream he couldn't figure out, he called Joseph. Joseph explained Pharaoh's dream. The Pharaoh was so thankful to Joseph that he made him a great leader in Egypt.

When Joseph was the ruler of Egypt, ten of his brothers came to him to buy food for their families. The brothers did not know this ruler was Joseph. But Joseph knew his brothers. He could have been angry and sent the brothers way. But instead, Joseph did a good work and forgave his brothers. He even gave them food and land so their whole family could move to Egypt and be with Joseph.

? discussion questions

1. Name one way Joseph did good work.
2. Name a way you can do good work today.

"Just Like Joseph" Mirror

![scissors icon]
What you need

- scissors or papercutter
- card stock
- aluminum foil
- crayons
- glue
- crayons or markers

![pencil icon]
What you do

1. For each child, photocopy and cut out a mirror on card stock. Older children may be able to cut for themselves.
2. Photocopy and cut out a Joseph for each child.
3. Trace around the center of the mirror for a pattern. Use the pattern to cut a foil mirror for each child.
4. Children color their mirrors and Josephs.
5. Children glue the foil to the card stock mirrors, and then glue the Josephs to the mirrors.
6. Sing the song to the tune of "Three Blind Mice." Children look in the mirror when the song lyrics are, "Just like Joseph."

What to Say

Sing this song with me!

**Just like Joseph,
Just like Joseph,
I want to be,
I want to be.**

**Like Joseph I'll do good works,
And help my family.
Just like Joseph,
I want to be,
Just like Joseph,
Just like Joseph.**

Guard Puppet

What you need

- scissors or papercutter
- gray construction paper
- crayons or markers
- paper lunch bags
- glue

What you do

1. For each child, photocopy this page and cut out a set of guard puppet pieces for each child. Older children may be able to cut for themselves.
2. Cut gray construction paper into ½×3-inch strips.
3. Children color the puppet pieces.
4. Assist each child in gluing the puppet pieces to paper lunch bags.
5. Demonstrate how to make a chain with six paper strips.
6. Assist the children in gluing the chains' ends in place on the puppets' hands.
7. Children practice the verse using their puppets.

What to Say

Just like a guard watches his prisoners, we should watch for opportunities to do good things. If you're supposed to make your bed each morning, don't miss a day of making your bed. Watch the trash can so you'll know when the bag is full and ready to be taken out. Be on guard to find ways to do good things!

A Story to Tell

What you need

- scissors or papercutter
- crayons or markers

What you do

1. For each child, photocopy this page and cut out Bible story boxes.
Older children may be able to cut for themselves.

2. Children number story pictures in order. The first one has been completed.

What to Say

Joseph was in prison. While there, Joseph told the king what his dreams meant. The king was pleased. He made Joseph an important man. Joseph was reunited with his family.

These pictures of Joseph are all mixed up. Can you number them in the correct order? The first one is done for you.

 Top 50 Creative Bible Lessons: Fun Activities for Preschoolers

Joseph in Prison

Doing Good Work (based on Genesis 37—50)

 memory verse

[God] has created us . . . so we can do the good things he planned for us. Ephesians 2:10

 discussion questions

1. Name one way Joseph did good work.

2. Name a way you can do good work today.

Joseph, Ruler of Egypt

Draw one or more of Joseph's brothers as they talk to him on the throne.

Miriam and Baby Moses

memory verse

Give all your worries and cares to God, for he cares about you. 1 Peter 5:7

Baby in a Basket (based on Exodus 2:1–10)

God's people were in the land of Egypt. Their families grew and grew.

The king, who was called *Pharaoh* said, "We must do something to keep these people from becoming so strong that they can rule over us." So, Pharaoh made God's people become their slaves. Then, Pharaoh said that all baby boys must be killed! He thought if he killed all the baby boys, God's people would die off and there would be no more of them.

Miriam and her family loved God. And Miriam was so excited! Her mother had just had a new baby boy. The whole family loved the baby, but they knew about Pharaoh's mean plan to kill the baby boys born to God's people.

Miriam did not want Pharaoh's men to find her new baby brother. She helped her mother hide him for as long as they could. When they could hide him no longer, Miriam's mother made a special basket and placed the baby in the basket. Then she placed the basket in the river. She prayed to God and trusted that God would protect the baby.

Miriam stayed and watched over the baby to make sure he was safe. Pharaoh's daughter found the basket. The princess named the baby Moses. Miriam asked the princess, "Would you like me to get someone to feed the baby for you?"

When Pharaoh's daughter said yes, Miriam went and got her mother. Moses' mommy got to help take care of him, and he was safe. Miriam and her family were so happy! And Baby Moses was safe.

 ### discussion questions

1. Why did Miriam and Moses' mother put Baby Moses in a basket?
2. How did God provide for Baby Moses to be safe and cared for?

Little Baby Boy

What you need

- none

What you do

1. Photocopy this page to use as reference as you teach the finger play to children.
2. Demonstrate the fun finger play below to help the children remember the Bible story of how Moses was saved with the help of his big sister Miriam.
3. Children perform the finger play with you as time and interest allow.

What to Say

Miriam had a new baby brother. She loved her baby brother very much, but he was in danger. Her mother had to hide him from Pharaoh, who wanted all the boy babies killed. Moses' mother hid him in a basket. Then she put the basket into the Nile River.

It was Miriam's job to watch the basket that she and her mother had made to see where it went. When the Pharaoh's own daughter found the baby, Miriam offered her mother to help care for the child. God protected and cared for this special baby boy. And God cares for you, too!

See the little baby boy,	*cup hands around eyes like binoculars*
Floating in the reeds	*make a floating motion with right hand*
Slowly down the river.	*continue the floating motion with left hand this time*
Who could this baby be?	*put both hands out, palms up as if asking a question*
For this is baby Moses;	*cradle arms*
God's promises he'll share.	*point up to Heaven*
When Pharaoh's daughter finds him,	*cup both hands together, palms up*
Miriam and her mother help with his care.	*cradle arms*

Where's the Baby?

What you need

- scissors
- crayons or markers
- glue

What you do

1. For each child, photocopy this page and cut out the picture and the figure of Baby Moses. Older children may be able to cut for themselves.
2. Children color the picture and the figure of the baby.
3. After coloring, children glue the baby in the basket.

What to Say

God cared for Baby Moses by giving him his own mother to take care of him. God cares for you, too!

"Give all your worries and cares to God, for he cares about you." 1 Peter 5:7

 Top 50 Creative Bible Lessons: Fun Activities for Preschoolers

Moses' Family Finger Puppets

What you need

- scissors or papercutter
- crayons or markers
- transparent tape

What you do

1. For each child, photocopy this page and cut out puppets. Older children may be able to cut for themselves.

2. Children color puppets.

3. Help children wrap their finger puppets around a finger. Make sure the fit is loose so it can be removed without tearing, and then use transparent tape to secure the ring.

Teaching Tip: Ahead of time, make a set to use as you tell the Bible story.

You can use your finger puppets to tell the story of Baby Moses to others!

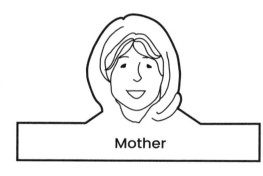

Mother

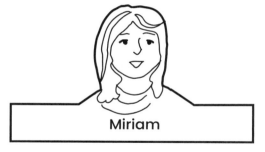

Miriam

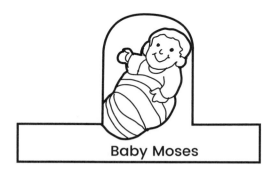

Baby Moses

Princess

Miriam and Baby Moses

Baby in a Basket (based on Exodus 2:1–10)

memory verse

Give all your worries and cares to God, for he cares about you. 1 Peter 5:7

discussion questions

1. Why did Miriam and Moses' mother put Baby Moses in a basket?
2. How did God provide for Baby Moses to be safe and cared for?

Princess Rescues a Baby

Follow the path to help the Egyptian princess find baby Moses in the reeds

Moses Leads God's People

memory verse

God is awesome . . . Praise be to God! Psalm 68:35

God's Awesome Power (based on Exodus 3:1–15; 7—11, 12:31; 14; 20)

God's people were very sad. They had to work hard every day as slaves in Egypt. They cried and prayed to God, asking him to make a way for them to be free. God's people knew how awesome God is. They knew that God can do anything!

One day, one of God's people, a man named Moses, saw a bush. The bush was burning, but it wasn't burning up! God talked to Moses from the bush. God told Moses, "Go to Egypt." God explained to Moses that he had a big job for him to do. God wanted Moses to go to Egypt and tell the king, Pharaoh, to let all of his people free!

Moses was afraid to go to Egypt. He was afraid to talk to Pharaoh. But he knew God would help him. God is so awesome!

Moses told the king of Egypt, Pharaoh, "God says to let his people go!" Pharaoh was angry and said, "No! They will stay my slaves!" Every time Pharoah said no, God used his awesome power to send something bad to encourage him to change his mind—like tons of frogs; bugs, bugs, and more bugs; sores on the bodies; and so on. Each time, no matter what bad thing happened, Pharaoh kept telling Moses, "No!"

So God sent his last warning. Pharaoh's oldest son died, along with all the other firstborn sons of humans and animals. Pharaoh had enough. He let Moses and the people leave.

After God's people had left, Pharaoh changed his mind! He chased Moses and his people. When the people saw a huge sea (called the Red Sea) in front of them, they got scared. But Moses told the people not to be afraid. "God will help us!" he said. And God did! He did one of the most awesome and spectacular things he ever did! God made the water in the middle separate! The people crossed onto dry land. Then God closed the sea so the soldiers could not cross. God took care of Moses and his people, and he takes care of us.

discussion questions

1. What was burning at the beginning of our story?
2. Name one of the awesome things God did to help his people.

Bush Burning Bright

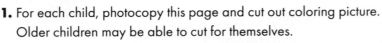

What you need

- scissors or papercutter
- crayons or markers, variety of colors but with extra red and orange

What you do

1. For each child, photocopy this page and cut out coloring picture. Older children may be able to cut for themselves.

2. Children color all of the diamonds red and the triangles orange; then they color the rest of the picture.

What to Say

When Moses saw the burning bush, he was amazed! The bush was burning, but it wasn't burning up! Then something even more awesome and amazing happened: God talked to Moses from the bush. God told Moses, "Go to Egypt." Moses was afraid to go, but he knew God would help him. Moses knew with our awesome God helping him, there wasn't anything he couldn't do!

Frog Name Tag

What you need

- scissors or papercutter
- crayons or markers
- spring-type clothespins
- glue
- large wiggle eyes

What you do

1. For each child, photocopy this page and cut out a frog for each child. Older children may be able to cut for themselves.

2. Children color the frogs. Assist them in writing their names on the line.

3. Show how to glue the wiggle eyes to the frog.

4. Demonstrate how to tape the frog to the clothespin.

5. When glue dries, assist in clipping the frog to the childrens' clothes.

What to Say

In our story today there are frogs—hundreds of frogs! When you hear me say the word, "frog," say, "ribbit, ribbit."

Briefly tell the plague section of today's story, with lots of emphasis on the frogs!

Crossing the Red Sea

What you need

- scissors or papercutter
- crayons or markers

What you do

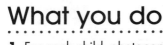

1. For each child, photocopy this page and cut out the maze. Older children may be able to cut for themselves.

2. Children follow the path with a crayon or marker.

3. Children color the picture.

What to Say

Pharaoh changed his mind! His army chased Moses and God's people. When the people saw the huge Red Sea in front of them, they got scared. But Moses knew how awesome and powerful God is. Moses told the people not to be afraid. "God will help us!" he said. And God did! He parted the sea! The people crossed on dry land, safely to the other side. God used his awesome power to take care of Moses and his people. God uses his awesome power to help us, too.

 Top 50 Creative Bible Lessons: Fun Activities for Preschoolers

Moses Leads God's People

God's Awesome Power (based on Exodus 3:1–15; 7—11, 12:31; 14; 20)

memory verse

God is awesome . . . Praise be to God! Psalm 68:35

discussion questions

1. What was burning at the beginning of our story?

2. Name one of the awesome things God did to help his people.

Ten Rules to Obey

Connect the dots to see where we can read God's rules.

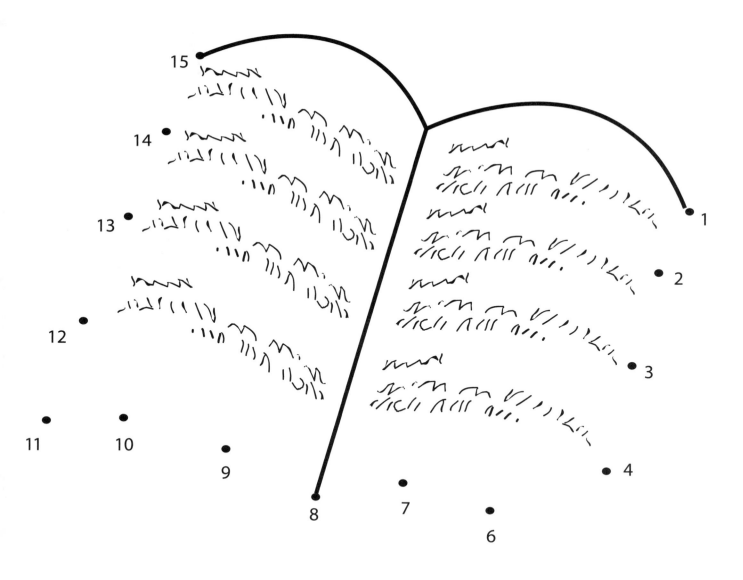

Joshua Is Brave

memory verse

Do not fear. Isaiah 35:4

Don't Be Afraid (based on Joshua 1:1–18)

The Israelites were wandering in the wilderness. God wanted his people to live in Canaan, but they would have to take the land from the Canaanites.

"We're afraid. There are giants in that land," said one of the spies who had been sent to check out the land.

"That's right," said another spy. "We would be defeated."

Only two men, Joshua and Caleb, wanted to go fight the Canaanites. They knew God would be with them. But the people of Israel were afraid, so God punished them.

"You will wander in the wilderness for the rest of your lives. Only Joshua and Caleb, who believed I would be with them in war, will be brought into Canaan," said God.

When Moses, their leader, was dying, he called Joshua. "It is time for me to die. You will be the new leader. Take the people and go into Canaan. Don't be afraid. God will be with you."

When Moses died, God spoke to Joshua. "I want you to go and win the war against Canaan," he said. "Every place you walk I will give to my people."

Joshua knelt in the presence of God. "Yes, Lord."

Again God spoke. "I will be with you all the days of your life. I will never fail you or leave you. Make sure you read and obey the law I have written, and I will be with you wherever you go."

Joshua went to his people and told them what God said. "God has given us a beautiful land to live in. It is Canaan—the land where wonderful crops will grow. The land has beautiful flowers blooming everywhere and strong, tall trees. We must go and possess the land. God wants us to be strong and not be afraid."

"Yes," agreed the people of Israel. "We will go. Whatever you say to us, we will do. We will not be afraid."

God gave Joshua and his people the land because they obeyed him and were not afraid.

 discussion questions

1. What are things kids your age might be afraid of?
2. How can God help you to be brave?

Glitter Verse

What you need

- scissors or papercutter
- glue in squeeze bottles
- glitter
- construction paper

What you do

1. For each child, photocopy and cut out a verse label. Older children may be able to cut for themselves.

2. Cut a piece of construction paper 1 inch larger than the verse on all four sides.

3. Glue a verse to a construction paper rectangle for each child.

4. Show how to trace the verse with glue, one letter at a time, and then sprinkle with glitter.

DO NOT FEAR.
Isaiah 35:4

10 Marching Soldiers

What you need

- crayons or markers
- scissors or papercutter
- spring-type clothespins
- glue

What you do

1. Before class, photocopy and cut out a badge for each child. Older children may be able to cut for themselves.
2. Children color the badges.
3. Assist in gluing a clothespin to the back of the badge. Clip the pin to the child's clothes.
4. Sing the song to the tune of "Ten Little Indians" while marching in place. If you have an open space, march in a circle.

What to Say

Sing this song with me!

1 marching, 2 marching, 3 marching soldiers,
4 marching, 5 marching, 6 marching soldiers,
7 marching, 8 marching, 9 marching soldiers,
10 soldiers march to war.

Night-Time Fright

What you need

- scissors or papercutter
- black construction paper
- glue
- white crayons or markers
- gold stars

What you do

1. Before class, photocopy this page for each child and cut out the activity box. Older children may be able to cut for themselves.

2. Cut pieces of black construction paper to fit the activity sheet.

3. Show the children where to glue the construction paper to the worksheet.

4. Children use the white crayon to draw a picture of themselves in the dark.

5. Children stick stars in the darkness.

What to Say

You may find the dark scary, but who is with you even in the dark?
(God) **What does God tell us about fear?** (Do not fear.)

GLUE BLACK HERE

"Do not fear."
Isaiah 35:4

Joshua Is Brave

Don't Be Afraid (based on Joshua 1:1–18)

memory verse
Do not fear. Isaiah 35:4

discussion questions
1. What are things kids your age might be afraid of?
2. How can God help you to be brave?

Marching to Canaan

Follow the marching footsteps from the wilderness to Canaan. Trace the route with your finger or a crayon.

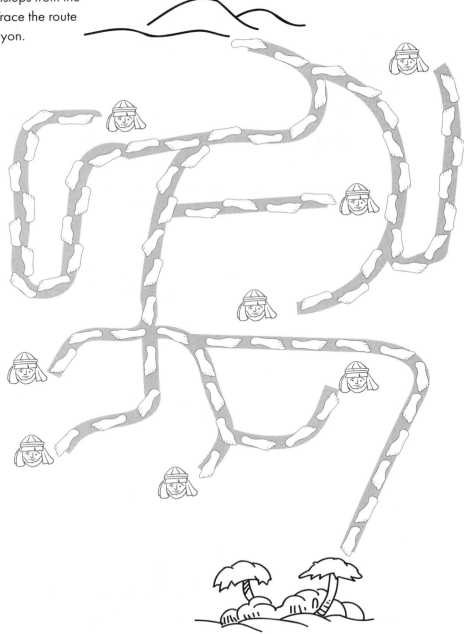

Mighty Samson

memory verse

Your word is a lamp to guide my feet and a light for my path. Psalm 119:105

Guidance for Samson (based on Judges 13; 14:5–6; 15:14–16; 16)

Before Samson was born, an angel told his mother and father that Samson would be a very special son who would do the work of the Lord. The angel gave Samson's parents guidance from God for raising Samson. They were told to make sure he ate special foods and to never cut his hair. The Lord blessed Samson and made him really strong.

Samson killed a lion with his bare hands! Once Samson fought a thousand Philistines and won. Another time he carried away a whole city gate. God guided Samson to save the Israelites from their enemies.

Samson began to be careless in his love for God. As a result, he made some very bad choices. Samson met a woman, Delilah, and forgot about looking to God for guidance. Delilah didn't love God, and she was getting close to Samson so she could help his enemies defeat him!

Delilah asked Samson the secreat of his great strength. Samson said that God had told him never to cut his hair for that was the secret of his strength. Delilah helped Samson's enemies, the Philistines, cut off his hair. After the haircut, Samson's strength was gone! His enemies then poked out his eyes and threw him into prison.

While Samson was in prison, his hair grew back. One day the Philistines had a party in the temple. The party was for one of their fake gods. They brought Samson to the party to laugh at him. Samson prayed, "God, please give me strength one more time." Samson pushed against the pillars that held up the building. The pillars crumbled and the temple collapsed. The wicked men died, along with Samson.

discussion questions

1. What was Samson never supposed to cut off?
2. What happened when Samson's hair was cut off?

Following God

What you need

- scissors
- hole punch
- yarn
- transparent tape
- crayons or markers

What you do

1. On card stock, photocopy and cut out a shoe for each child. Older children may be able to cut for themselves. Punch holes as indicated. Cut an 18-inch length of yarn for each child and wrap tape tightly around one end like the end of a shoestring. Tape the other end to the back of the shoe.

2. Say, **Our verse says that God's Word, the Bible, is like a light for our feet. That means God guides us to live the very best life. It's up to us to listen and follow. The shoes we're making are reminders to follow God's Word.**

3. Children color shoes.

4. Demonstrate how to lace the shoes by sewing the yarn through the holes, beginning with the hole closest to the toes. Instead of going in and out of the holes in a running stitch, whip stitch by inserting the yarn from the back for each hole.

5. After the fourth hole, trim yarn and tape to the back of the shoe.

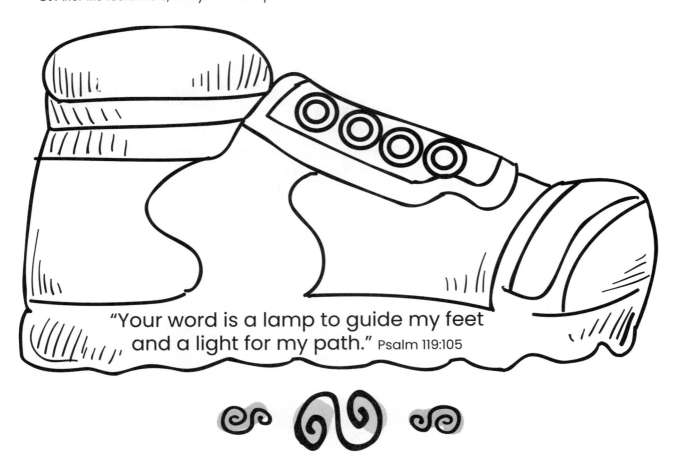

"Your word is a lamp to guide my feet and a light for my path." Psalm 119:105

 Top 50 Creative Bible Lessons: Fun Activities for Preschoolers

Lion Snack

What you need

- bread
- round cookie cutters, small bowl, or plastic drinking glass
- soft margarine
- shredded cheese
- raisins

What you do

1. Help the children cut a circle from a piece of bread, using a round cookie cutter, or the open end of a bowl or plastic drinking glass.
2. Help the children spread margarine on the bread.
3. Show how to make lion faces by placing raisins for eyes, nose, and mouth and shredded cheese around the edge for the mane.

What to Say

In our story today we heard that Samson was so strong, he was able to kill a lion with his bare hands! Samson was strong because God promised that as long as Samson followed his commands, he would be a strong and mighty leader of God's people.

God wants to guide us, too. When we listen to God's Word and follow him, we will live the very best life—the life God has planned for us.

Samson Mask

What you need

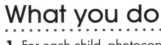

- sheets of brown paper
- scissors
- 6-inch paper plates, one for each child
- glue
- jumbo craft sticks, one for each child
- masking tape
- crayons or markers

What you do

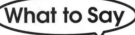

1. For each child, photocopy this page onto brown paper. Cut out the beards. Older children may be able to cut beards for themselves. Cut eye holes in the paper plates for children. (Note: Make sure eye holes are approximately 1½–2 inches wide.)
2. Children glue beards to the botton backside of a paper plate.
3. From brown-paper scraps or additional sheets, children cut strips for hair and glue them to the paper plate.
4. Children tape a jumbo craft stick to the back of the plate to make a handle for their mask.

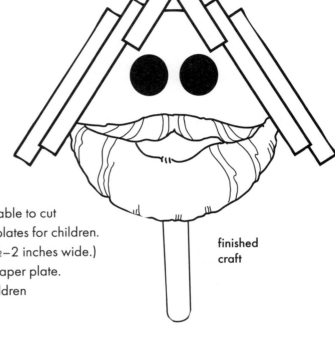

finished craft

What to Say

We can use our masks to pretend we are Samson before his hair was cut. Our masks show a smile because Samson was following God's commands, and that makes us happy. Before his hair was cut, Samson was super strong! Let's pretend to be strong, too. Show me your muscles!

Mighty Samson

Guidance for Samson (based on Judges 13; 14:5–6; 15:14–16; 16)

 memory verse
....
Your word is a lamp to guide my feet and a light for my path. Psalm 119:105

 discussion questions
....
1. What was Samson never supposed to cut off?

2. What happened when Samson's hair was cut off?

Samson Is Strong Again

Draw hair, a moustache, and a beard on Samson.

Ruth and Naomi Thank God

memory verse

Give thanks to [God]. Psalm 100:4

Thank You, Thank You! (based on Ruth 1; 2:8–17; 4:13–17)

Naomi and her husband had two sons. They moved far away from home because they needed to find food.

After a few years, Naomi's husband died. One of Naomi's sons married Orpah and the other married Ruth. After 10 years, the sons died also.

Naomi wanted to go back to her family in her hometown, Bethlehem. She told Orpah and Ruth to go back to their own families and find new husbands. But Ruth loved Naomi. She didn't want to leave Naomi alone.

Ruth went with Naomi back to Bethlehem. She said, "Where you go I will go. Your God will be my God."

Ruth knew she needed to find a way to provide food for herself and Naomi. "Naomi, don't you worry about our food," Ruth told her. "It's the time of barley harvest. I'll go to the fields tomorrow and gather whatever barley is left."

A relative of Naomi named Boaz owned the fields where Ruth went to pick the barley. He had heard how kind she had been to travel a long distance with Naomi and take care of her.

"Come and eat our food for lunch," said Boaz. "You will be safe here, and you may gather all the barley you need."

Ruth's heart was happy because of Boaz's kindness. "Thank you, thank you," she told him.

That night, when Ruth told Naomi what Boaz had said, Naomi said, "Praise God for taking care of us!"

As time went by, Boaz married Ruth. They had a baby boy named Obed. Naomi was so happy to have a grandson to love! They were all so thankful to God for providing so many good things to their family.

? discussion questions

1. What has God done for you that you are thankful for?

2. How can we show our thanks to God? To others?

Helping Ruth

What you need

- scissors or papercutter
- two baskets
- empty box

What you do

1. Photocopy this page and cut out the food cards. You will need two sets of cards.
2. Divide children into two teams, lining the teams in single-file position.
3. Choose one child from each team to be Ruth or Boaz. Ruth/Boaz should sit on the ground about ten feet away from the line with a basket in her lap.
4. Place the food cards in a box between the two teams.
5. At the go signal, the first in line should grab a food card, run to Ruth/Boaz and say, **"I am thankful for** [name of food on card]," drop the card in the basket, and run back to tag the hand of the next person in line. Continue until one team finishes with all their cards.
6. The first team to finish tells a reason they are thankful to God.

Optional: Color, or ask kids who arrive early to color, the cards.

Ruth's Reward

What you need

- scissors or papercutter
- flannel
- ruler
- crayons or markers
- glue

What you do

1. Photocopy this page and cut out the trophy cup, baby Obed figure, and Ruth and Boaz figures. Older children may be able to cut for themselves. Fold trophy on dashed line. Cut flannel into 3×3-inch squares, one for each child.
2. Children color tropies, baby Obed figure, and Ruth and Boaz figure.
3. Children open trophies and glue Ruth and Boaz figure inside.
4. Children each glue a fabric square around the baby Obed figure as a blanket and then glue the wrapped baby into Ruth's arms.

What to Say

We often give trophies to say thanks to people who do great things. Ruth did something great by taking care of Naomi. Let's make a trophy for Ruth!

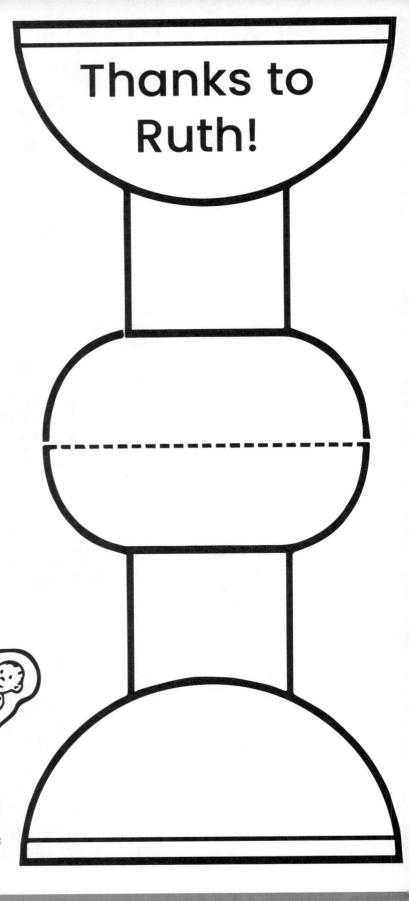

Thanks to Ruth!

 Top 50 Creative Bible Lessons: Fun Activities for Preschoolers

Ruth and Naomi Coloring Page

What you need

- scissors or papercutter
- crayons or markers

What you do

1. Photocopy this page and cut out the coloring picture. Older children may be able to cut for themselves.
2. Children color the picture.

What to Say

Ruth and Naomi were thankful to have each other. Ruth was thankful to have Naomi's motherly love and good advice. Naomi was thankful to have Ruth's company. Naomi was also thankful that Ruth gathered food for them to eat. Ruth and Naomi were both thankful to God that he gave them each other.

Top 50 Creative Bible Lessons: Fun Activities for Preschoolers.

Ruth and Naomi Thank God

Thank You, Thank You! (based on Ruth 1; 2:8–17; 4:13–17)

memory verse

Give thanks to [God]. Psalm 100:4

discussion questions

1. What has God done for you that you are thankful for?
2. How can we show our thanks to God? To others?

Song and Verse

Sing "Wherever You Go" with the children to the tune of "B-I-N-G-O."

Say the "Good Friend" verse with your children. Clap hands together every time you say the word "friend."

Wherever You Go

Ruth told Naomi, "I am your friend,
And I'll go where you go."
"Wherever you will go,
Wherever you will go,
Wherever you will go,
I will go there, too."

Good Friend

Good friend.
Good friend.
I thank God for good friends.
I can help my friends.

Good friend.
Good friend.
I thank God for good friends.
I'll share with my friends.

Good friend.
Good friend.
I thank God for good friends.
I will love my friends.

Samuel Listens

memory verse

Listen carefully to the voice of the LORD your God. Exodus 15:26

Speak, Lord (based on 1 Samuel 1—2:11,18–21,26; 3:1–19)

There was a woman named Hannah who loved God very much. There was one thing that made Hannah very sad. She very much wanted a baby, but had been unable to have one.

One day at the tabernacle, Hannah prayed and asked God to give her a baby. She promised that she would take her child to God's house, the tabernacle. God heard Hannah's prayer and gave her a son. Hannah named him *Samuel*, which means "God hears."

When Samuel was old enough, Hannah kept her promise and took him to the tabernacle to live with the priest, Eli. Samuel loved God. Samuel also loved God's house. Samuel grew up in the tabernacle. He was a good boy. Samuel obeyed Eli, the priest.

One night when Samuel was sleeping, he heard his name called. He ran to Eli because he thought Eli called him. After Samuel heard his name called and ran to Eli three times, Eli realized it was God who was calling Samuel.

The fourth time the Lord called Samuel, he said, "Speak, Lord. Your servant is listening." God told Samuel some things he planned to do.

After that, God often talked with Samuel. Samuel always listened and did what God wanted him to do. Samuel became a priest and was the leader of God's people for many years.

Samuel was a good leader because he listened to and obeyed God. We should listen to God, too.

discussion questions

1. Why did Samuel live in the tabernacle?

2. Who called for Samuel in the middle of the night?

A Mother's Promise

What you need

- scissors or papercutter
- crayons or markers

What you do

1. Photocopy this page and cut out the maze. Older children may be able to cut for themselves.
2. Children follow the path with a crayon or marker to help Hannah and Samuel find their way to the Tabernacle.

What to Say

Hannah promised that if God gave her a son, she would take him to God's house, the tabernacle, to live. God heard Hannah's prayer and gave her a son, named Samuel. When Samuel was old enough, Hannah kept her promise. She took him to the tabernacle. God rewards those who keep their promises to him.

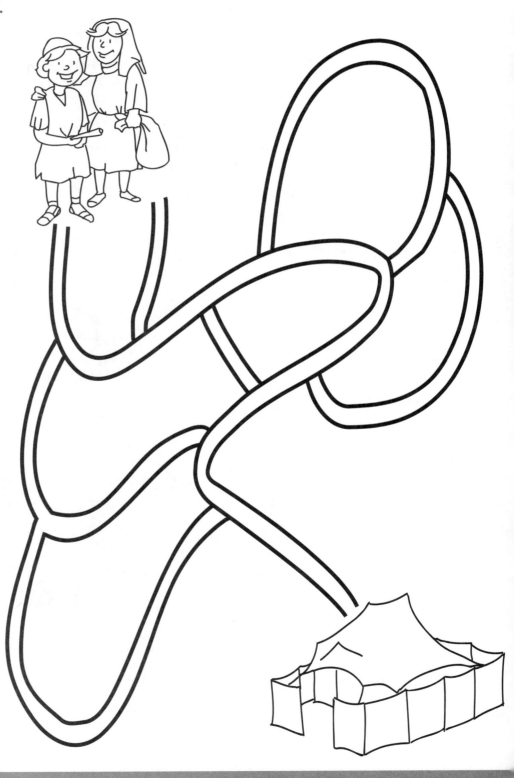

Helping in the Temple

What you need

- scissors or papercutter
- craft straw or rafia
- crayons or markers
- small bowls
- glue

What you do

1. Photocopy this page and cut out the coloring picture. Older children may be able to cut for themselves. Cut approximately 1-inch pieces of craft straw and place in small bowls, one bowl for every three or four children.
2. Children color the picture of Samuel working in the temple and draw a smile on his face.
3. Children glue cut straw to the end of the broom.

What to Say

When Samuel lived in the temple with the priest, Eli, he helped by keeping the floors clean and lighting the lamps. He did whatever Eli asked him to do because this was a way to show he was listening to Eli—and to God!

God tells us to obey our parents. When you do what your parents say, you show that you're listening to them and also listening to God!

I Can Listen to God

What you need

- none

What you do

1. Photocopy this page to use as reference as you teach the finger play to children.
2. Demonstrate the fun finger play below to help the children remember the Bible story of Samuel.
3. Children perform the finger play with you as time and interest allows.

What to Say

Once Samuel realized that God had something to say to him, he was ready to listen. Samuel wanted to always be ready to listen to God. Even when Samuel was a young child, God talked to him. Did Samuel know that it was God talking to him at first? What do you think God sounds like?

1 – 2 – 3

Hold up three fingers, one at a time.

I stretch up big and tall.

Stretch your arms way above your head.

I grow and grow,

Stand up on your tiptoes.

So big you know,

Hold your arms straight out to your sides.

As I listen for God's call.

Hold your hands up to your ears as if listening.

Samuel Listens

Speak, Lord (based on 1 Samuel 1—2:11,18–21,26; 3:1–19)

memory verse

Listen carefully to the voice of the Lord your God. Exodus 15:26

discussion questions

1. Why did Samuel live in the tabernacle?

2. Who called for Samuel in the middle of the night?

Samuel Hears God's Call

Samuel loved God. Samuel also loved God's house. One night God talked to Samuel. God told Samuel some things he planned to do. Samuel listened and obeyed God. We should listen to God, too.

In the picture below, find the hidden objects: an oil lamp, a water pitcher, a lamb, a scroll, and a patched robe.

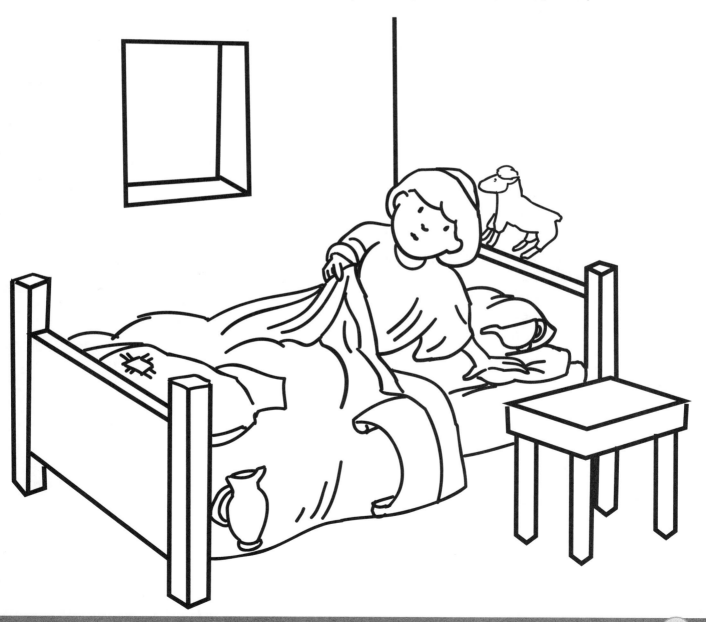

David the Shepherd Boy

memory verse

Trust in the LORD and do good. Psalm 37:3

David Trusts God (based on 1,2 Samuel, 1 Chronicles)

There was a young shepherd named David who had a good heart and loved God. David learned at a very early age to trust in the Lord. As a shepherd, he was constantly protecting his sheep and himself from dangerous animals. David knew that the Lord would take care of him.

While David was at home tending the family sheep, three of his older brothers were away helping King Saul fight a war against the Philistines. David's father asked him to take some supplies to his brothers and to make sure that they were all right. No matter where David was, he knew he could call upon God to help keep him safe. David trusted God.

When David got to his brothers, he heard one of the Philistines speaking against God. This man was a giant named Goliath. Goliath was challenging God's people to fight him. Even though David was very young, he knew that the giant Goliath must not be allowed to torment God's people any longer

David knew what he had to do. David trusted that God could keep him safe and help him defeat the giant.

David took five small stones from a nearby stream. He said to Goliath, "You have your spear, but I have the Lord God with me! God doesn't need a sword or a spear. God will win the battle!"

David placed one stone in his slingshot, took aim, and . . . WHAP! The stone hit Goliath right between the eyes. Goliah fell down, and the Philistine army ran away! David was a hero because he trusted God!

? discussion questions

1. What animal did David take care of for his family?
2. What did David use to beat Goliath and the other Philistines?

David's Sheep

What you need

- scissors or papercutter
- crayons or markers

What you do

1. Photocopy this page and cut out the coloring picture. Older children may be able to cut for themselves.

2. Children color the picture according to the following code:

Spaces with A = white; with B = green; with C = blue; with D = brown; with E = black.

What to Say

David watched his father's sheep. He took very good care of them. When the people needed a new king, God picked David. David made a good king because he trusted God.

Count to Five

What you need

- scissors or papercutter
- crayons or markers

What you do

1. Photocopy this page and cut out the counting activity. Older children may be able to cut for themselves.

2. Lead children to point to and count the five stones a few times.

3. Children then follow the number outlines to write the numbers, and then color the stones.

What to Say

David was a young shepherd boy who stayed at home and helped his father tend their sheep while his older brothers went off to battle. While visiting his brothers, David was called by God to defeat the army's greatest enemy, Goliath. David was able to do this by trusting in God and relying on God's power.

Trust Stones

What you need

- scissors or papercutter
- crayons or markers
- smooth stones
- cotton swabs
- glue

What you do

1. Photocopy this page several times and cut out the happy faces and stars. Older children may be able to cut for themselves. Gather smooth stones, five for each child. (If the weather permits, children find their own stones.)
2. Children color the happy faces and stars.
3. Using a cotton swab, children paint white glue on the rocks and then place a happy face or star on the rock.

For Younger Children: Provide happy face and star stickers for children to use.

 **What to Say**

Because David trusted God and had faith in him, he knew he could defeat Goliath. With faith, we can "Trust in the LORD and do good" (Psalm 37:3). **God gave David the courage to face Goliath! How many stones did it take to win? Let's count to five together: 1, 2, 3, 4, 5! Take home your Trust Stones to remind you to have trust in God.**

David the Shepherd Boy

David Trusts God (based on 1,2 Samuel, 1 Chronicles)

 memory verse

Trust in the LORD and do good. Psalm 37:3

 discussion questions

1. What animal did David take care of for his family?

2. What did David use to beat Goliath and the other Philistines?

David and His Sheep

Color the picture of David and his sheep. Bend and glue a piece of a pipe cleaner on David's staff and glue cotton balls on the sheep.

David Is Kind

memory verse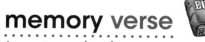

Love is . . . kind. 1 Corinthians 13:4

David Shows Love to Mephibosheth (based on 2 Samuel 9)

King David's best friend was Jonathan, King Saul's son. When the two were young men, they promised that they would always be friends. David also promised Jonathan that he would always take care of Jonathan's family.

Jonathan was killed in a battle with the Philistines. But King David was so busy taking care of his nation that he forgot his promise to Jonathan.

When he remembered, David instructed his men to find Jonathan's family. They found Jonathan's son, Mephibosheth, who was not able to walk because of an accident when he was a baby. Mephibosheth had grown up and married, but he lived with his family far away from other people. He didn't want people to be mean to him because of his handicap.

Mephibosheth was frightened when David invited him to the palace. He knew his grandfather, Saul, had been mean to David. Mephibosheth thought David might want to kill the other family members.

When he got to the palace, Mephibosheth bowed down before the king. He shook with fear.

"Don't be afraid," David told him. "Your father was my best friend. I won't harm you. I will give you all the land that belonged to Saul, your grandfather. I will give you everything you need."

Mephibosheth had lived away from people so long that he was shy. He felt unworthy of the honor King David was giving him. "Thank you, King David," Mephibosheth said, bowing once more. "Thank you for your kindness."

Mephibosheth lived in comfort, enjoying the land, herds, and flocks King David gave to him. "King David loved my father," Mephibosheth said, "and with that love he showed kindness to me."

discussion questions

1. Why did David want to be kind to Mephibosheth?

2. How can you show kindness to your friends?

BEE-ing Kind Flower

What you need

- scissors
- crayons or markers
- plastic drinking straws
- tape
- glue
- bee stickers

What you do

1. Photocopy two flowers and a leaf for each child and cut them out. Older children may be able to cut for themselves.
2. Children color the flowers and leaves.
3. Assist each child in taping a straw to the back of one flower and gluing the back of the other flower to the taped side of the first flower.
4. Children fold the leaf around the straw and then glue in place.
5. Give each child a bee sticker to place on one of the flower petals.

Optional: Have each child make two flowers so the children can give one away and keep the other.

What to Say

The flower can remind us to be kind to others. Also, we can show kindness by giving our flowers to cheer neighbors or friends.

"Love . . . is kind." 1 Corinthians 13:4

King David's Table

What you need

- scissors or papercutter
- glue
- crayons or markers

What you do

1. For each child, photocopy and cut out the scene, the food pictures, and Mephibosheth. Older children may be able to cut some of the shapes for themselves.

2. Children color the pictures.

3. Children glue the food on the table.

4. Show the children where to glue Mephibosheth.

Mephibosheth at King David's table.
(2 Samuel 9:1–13)

Kingly Crown

What you need

- white card stock
- scissors
- colored foil or metallic card stock
- hole punch
- string, yarn, or ribbon
- crayons or markers
- glue

What you do

1. For each child, photocopy and cut out the crown from white card stock. Older children may be able to cut crowns for themselves. Photocopy the jewel patterns and use them to cut jewels from colored foil or metallic card stock. Cut 6- to 8-inch lengths of string, yarn, or ribbon. Punch holes at both sides of the crown as indicated.

2. Children color the crowns and then glue on the jewels you prepared.

3. Tie a string through the holes in each crown. Tie the crown around the child's head.

What to Say

King David was kind to Mephibosheth. He even let Mephibosheth wear his crown! Wearing our crowns can remind us to be kind to others. Being kind is a way to show God's love!

David Is Kind

David Shows Love to Mephibosheth (based on 2 Samuel 9)

memory verse

Love is . . . kind. 1 Corinthians 13:4

discussion questions

1. Why did David want to be kind to Mephibosheth?

2. How can you show kindness to your friends?

Color by Number

Color the picture using the color key.

For more craft fun, center the picture on a sheet of construction paper and attach with smiley stickers at all four corners.

1. red	2. blue
3. green	4. yellow
5. black	6. tan

God Takes Care of Elijah

memory verse

God has given us everything we need. 2 Peter 1:3

God Provides Food (based on 1 Kings 17:1–24)

God told Elijah a big secret. He said, "There will be no rain for a few years. It will not rain again until I make it rain. People will have trouble finding food and water.

"I want to take care of you. This is what I want you to do. Leave here and hide in the Kerith Ravine, east of the Jordan River. I will send ravens to feed you, and there is a river with water for you to drink."

Elijah obeyed God. He went to the Kerith Ravine, east of the Jordan River. While he stayed there, God sent ravens to feed him. The ravens brought Elijah bread and meat in the morning. The ravens brought Elijah bread and meat in the evening. Elijah drank water from the river.

God took care of Elijah.

Another time, Elijah was tired and hungry. God told him, "Go to the town. There is a poor widow who will give you food." When Elijah found the woman, he asked her for food.

The woman said, "I have only a little oil and a little flour to make one last cake of bread for my son and me, then we will starve." But the poor woman shared the bread with Elijah.

Can you guess what happened? As she poured out the flour, more flour was in her jar. Each day there was plenty of flour and oil. The widow and her son never went hungry again.

I'm so glad that God takes care of us!

discussion questions

1. Where did Elijah get water to drink?
2. How did Elijah get food?

Craft Stick Puppets

What you need

- scissors or papercutter
- two craft sticks (or straws)
- tape

What you do

1. Copy the page for each child and cut out the scene. Older children may be able to cut for themselves.
2. Cut out the two ravens and the Elijah figure.
3. Tape a craft stick to the back of the two ravens and the Elijah figure.
4. To tell the story, start with the Elijah puppet. As God talks to Elijah, move him a little. Then take Elijah on a trip. Let Elijah rest beside the river. Fly the raven puppets back and forth to bring Elijah food.

Flying Ravens Mobile

What you need

- scissors or papercutter
- construction paper
- paper plates
- crayons or markers
- tape or stapler
- narrow ribbon pieces, about 8- to 10-inches long

What you do

1. Copy this page for each child. Cut out the ravens and cut four 1×8-inch strips of construction paper for each child. Older children may be able to cut for themselves. Write on the center of the paper plates: "God sent ravens with food for Elijah."
2. Have the children color the ravens.
3. Evenly tape or staple the four paper strips to the edge of a paper plate for each child.
4. Tape a raven to the other end of each construction paper strip.
5. Poke two holes in the center of the plate and thread and tie a ribbon hanger.
6. Show how to turn the plate around until the ribbon is wound. Then have the children let go and watch it spin, making the ravens fly.

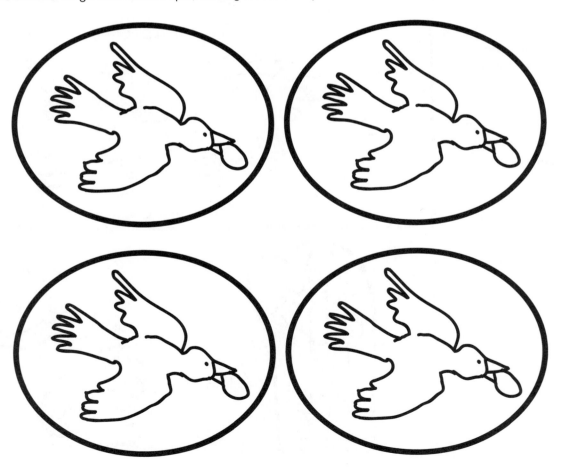

Everything We Need

What you need

- scissors or papercutter
- crayons or markers

What you do

1. Photocopy this page and cut out activity. Older children may be able to cut for themselves.
2. Children color pictures.
3. Children draw a square around the jar and bowl below that are EMPTY and draw a circle around the ones that are FULL.

"God has given us everything we need."

2 Peter 1:3

God Takes Care of Elijah

God Provides Food (based on 1 Kings 17:1–24)

memory verse

God has given us everything we need. 2 Peter 1:3

discussion questions

1. Where did Elijah get water to drink?

2. How did Elijah get food?

Surprise Picture

Use a brown crayon to fill in every space that contains the letter B. Use any color crayon you want to color any space with a dot (•). Do not color any space that has a *W* in it.

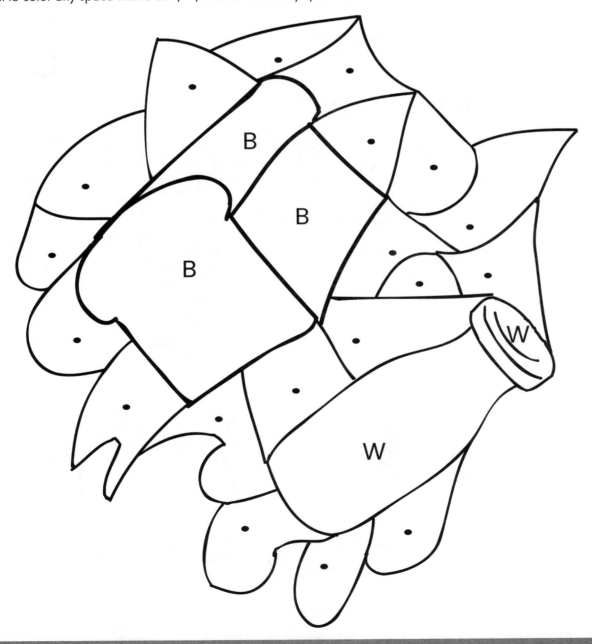

Jonah's Journey

memory verse

God our Savior . . . wants everyone to be saved. 1 Timothy 2:3–4

Jonah Preaches (based on Jonah 1—3)

Jonah was a prophet of God. It was his job to tell people messages from God. God had a message for Jonah to give to the people of Ninevah. So God told Jonah to go to Nineveh and tell them to stop doing bad things. They were to love God and do good things instead.

But Jonah didn't like the people in Ninevah. He didn't want the people in Ninevah to love and obey God. So Jonah hopped on a boat and went in the opposite direction!

God was not pleased with Jonah. He sent a HUGE storm. The sailors on the boat Jonah was sailing in did everything they could to save the ship. They ran to Jonah and asked him to pray for God's help. Jonah told them that it was his fault, and they would have to throw him into the sea.

The sailors didn't want to throw Jonah overboard, but when they realized it was their last chance, they did as Jonah asked, and the storm stopped!

God then sent a big fish to swallow Jonah. Jonah sat inside the smelly belly of the big fish. He prayed a lot. He thought about how he had disobeyed God. After three days the fish spat Jonah out onto the beach. Jonah had learned his lesson. He obeyed God and headed for Nineveh.

Jonah told the people of Nineveh that God was not happy with them. The people there worshiped false gods instead of the one true God. The people of Ninevah listened to Jonah. They changed and worshiped God instead. Because Jonah told them about God, the people of Nineveh were able to recieve God's forgiveness and be saved from the punishment for sin.

Sin is the Bible word for doing wrong things. The Bible tells us that the punishment for sin is death (Romans 6:23), but that God forgives and saves us through his Son, Jesus. Jonah didn't like the people of Nineveh, but God loves everyone! God wants everyone to be saved.

 discussion questions

1. Why didn't Jonah want to go to Ninevah?

2. What happened that made the sailors throw Jonah into the sea?

In the Fish

What you need

- scissors or papercutter
- crayons or markers

What you do

1. Photocopy this page and cut out dot-to-dot. Older children may be able to cut for themselves.

2. Children connect the dots from 1 to 23.

3. Children draw wave lines and other fish the space provided.

What to Say

When Jonah decided he didn't want to tell the people of Ninevah about God's love, he ended up in the belly of a big fish! God loves everyone. He wants everyone to love him, too! That's why he needs people who know and love him to tell others about him. God wants everyone to know that they can become members of his family.

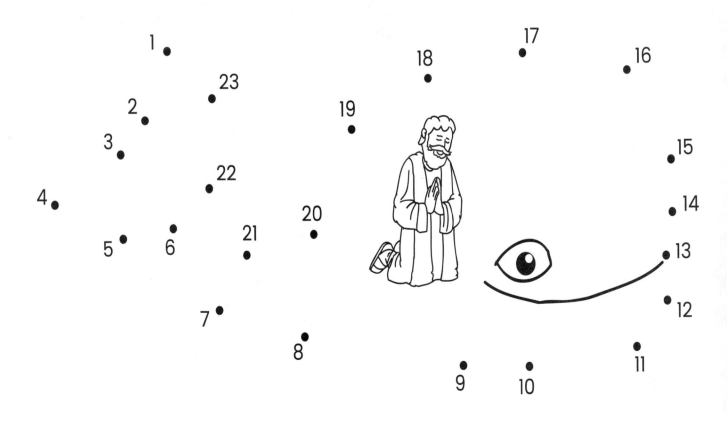

Memory Verse Necklace

What you need

- white card stock
- scissors
- hole punch
- yarn
- yard stick
- transparent tape
- pasta tubes (rigatoni, elbow macaroni, etc.)
- small bowls
- crayons or markers

What you do

1. On white card stock, photocopy this page and cut out circles. Older children may be able to cut for themselves. Punch holes where indicated.
2. Cut yarn into 36-inch lengths. With transparent tape, wrap one end of each yarn length to make it easier to thread circles onto yarn.
3. Put pasta tubes into small bowls, one for every two or three children.
4. Children color one set of circles.
5. Children thread circles and pasta tubes onto yarn length.
6. Tie ends of yarn in a knot to make a necklaces and place around children's necks.
7. Say, **Our necklaces remind us of today's verse!**

"God our Savior . . .

wants everyone

to be saved."

1 Timothy 2:3–4

On the Road Again

What you need

- scissors or papercutter
- crayons or markers

What you do

1. Photocopy this page and cut out maze. Older children may be able to cut for themselves.

2. Children use one color of crayon or marker to show Jonah's way to the ship.

3. Children use a second color to show how to go from the ship to the big fish.

4. Finally, children use a third color to find their way through the maze to the city of Ninevah.

What to Say

Instead of going straight to Ninevah like God wanted, Jonah first went on a ship. Then, from the ship he ended up inthe belly of a big fish! From the fish, Jonah fnially made his way to Ninevah!

Use a fourth crayon to show how Jonah could have gone straight to Ninevah.

Jonah's Journey

Jonah Preaches (based on Jonah 1—3)

memory verse

God our Savior . . . wants everyone to be saved. 1 Timothy 2:3–4

discussion questions

1. Why didn't Jonah want to go to Ninevah?

2. What happened that made the sailors throw Jonah into the sea?

Where's Jonah?

Nineveh was a crowded city. Jonah told the people to change their ways. Can you find Jonah in the crowd? A picture of Jonah's face is in the box to the right. Color Jonah. Then, color the rest of the picture. You can draw more people, too!

Jonah

Hezekiah Prays in the Temple

memory verse

Pray for each other. James 5:16

The Power of Prayer (based on 2 Kings 19)

King Hezekiah was a wise king who obeyed God's laws. He loved God. He wanted the people of his land to serve God only.

"I want all the altars of false gods destroyed," he said. After the altars were destroyed, he told the people, "God gave us the Ten Commandments to show us how he wants us to live. I want everyone to obey these laws."

There was a wicked king who wanted Hezekiah's land and its people. This king was from Assyria. He had a large army—much larger than King Hezekiah's army.

Hezekiah sent a letter to the Assyrian king. "Please send your army away," he said. "If you agree to leave my land, I will pay you any price."

The Assyrian king laughed to himself. He demanded that King Hezekiah send him large amounts of silver and gold. When the wicked king received the silver and gold, he ordered his soldiers to attack Jerusalem anyway.

"Tell King Hezekiah he must surrender," he instructed his soldiers.

Hezekiah was sad, but he knew God would help him. So he went to the temple to worship God.

After worshiping, King Hezekiah asked God to help the people of Jerusalem.

Then a prophet, Isaiah, told Hezekiah, "Don't be afraid. God sees how you worship him in his house. God will defend you and save the city."

That night, God's angel of death flew over the Assyrian camp, killing thousands of the soldiers. Hezekiah's kingdom was safe!

discussion questions

1. Where did King Hezekiah go when he was afraid?
2. What can we do when we are afraid?

Mystery Prayer

What you need

- crayons or markers

What you do

1. Photocopy this page for each child and cut out the color code. Older children may be able to cut for themselves.

2. Children color the picture using the following color code:

- cross = green
- star = yellow
- hash tag = blue
- smiley face = skin color

What to Say

In Bible days there were good kings and evil kings. What made the good kings different? (They loved God.) **How are we different when we love God?** (We are obedient, loving, helpful, kind, etc.) **One way we can show God we love him is by coming to worship him at church.**

"Pray for each other."
James 5:16

Prayer Reminder Clipboard

What you need

- card stock
- scissors or papercutter
- craft-foam sheets
- crayons or markers
- glue
- miniature spring-type clothespins
- magnets

What you do

1. Photocopy the patterns on card stock and cut out one set for each child. Older children may be able to cut for themselves. Cut a 2½×5-inch strip of craft foam for each child.

2. Children color verse card as well as boy and girl figures.

3. Instruct each child to glue the verse to the center of the foam strip, the boy and girl to the clothespins, and the clothespins to the foam strip on either side of the verse.

4. Give each child the two prayer cards to clip to the reminder.

5. Children glue the magnets to the backs of their reminders.

6. Ask the children whom they would like to pray for. Write the names on the prayer cards.

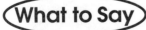 **What to Say**

Prayer is not limited to worship time at church. You can pray for your family and friends every day!

> "Pray for
> each other."
> James 5:16

Pray for	Pray for
_____	_____

Church Is Fun Book

What you need

- crayons or markers
- scissors or papercutter

What you do

1. Enlarging to 150 percent, photocopy a book for each child. Cut books out (around the thick outside line). Older children may be able to cut for themselves.
2. Children color their books.
3. Children fold the books in half lengthwise, then accordion-style, pressing the edges together firmly.

What to Say

Hezekiah worshiped God in the temple. We worship God at church! Let's make a book about all the things we do at church.

When we're done, we can practice sharing our book with each other. Later, we will take them home to share with our family and friends!

I worship with my friends.

I can pray to God when I worship.

I learn about Jesus when I worship.

I can invite my friends to worship with me.

I can sing songs when I worship.

I can give offerings when I worship.

Church is FUN!

I can praise God when I worship.

Hezekiah Prays in the Temple

The Power of Prayer (based on 2 Kings 19)

memory verse

Pray for each other. James 5:16

discussion questions

1. Where did King Hezekiah go when he was afraid?

2. What can we do when we are afraid?

A King's Treat

Gather together bread, butter, sugar, cinnamon, sprinkle container, and gem-shaped fruit snacks. Using the crown pattern below, cut a crown from bread for each family member. Mix sugar and cinnamon in a sprinkle container. Spread the bread crowns with butter. Place gem-shaped fruit snacks in a bowl.

Give a crown to each family member. Everyone takes turns sprinkling the crown with the cinnamon and sugar mixture and then uses gem-shaped fruit snacks to decorate their crowns.

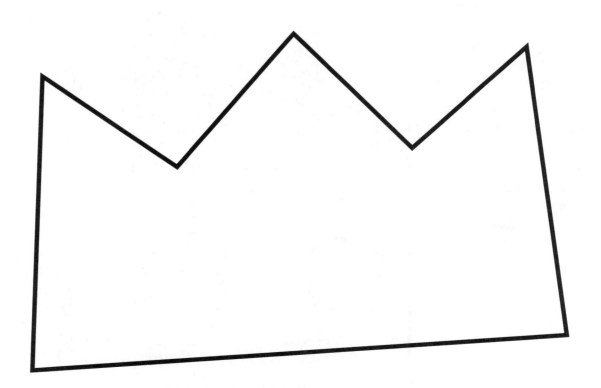

Josiah Respects God's Word

memory verse

Don't just listen to God's word. You must do what it says. James 1:22

The New King (based on 2 Chronicles 34:8–33)

Judah had a new king! The king was Josiah, and he was only eight years old. "I will need God's help," he said as they put the royal purple robe around his shoulders and the crown on his head. Josiah had loved God as long as he could remember, and he knew it was only God who could give him help.

One day Josiah called for one of his servants. "Our temple needs to be cleaned up," he said. "It has grown shabby, and we should not let the house of God get run down."

So the work on the temple began. One day, while working on the temple, the high priest found a scroll. He rushed to the royal scribe, Shaphan. "Shaphan, look what I have found," he said. "It is God's law, the only copy we have."

Shaphan took the scroll to the king. "Read to me what the law says," the king commanded.

As Shaphan read the words, the king started weeping. He tore his clothes in anguish and cried, "We have forgotten God's law. We are selfish and wicked. God must be angry with us."

God knew that Josiah was sorry for the laws they had been disobeying. "All will be well as long as Josiah lives," God promised.

When Josiah heard the promise of God, he called his people together and read to them the laws of God. "I promise to respect and obey the Word of God. Will you?" he asked.

"Yes, yes," said the people "We also promise to respect and obey God's Word.

Then all the people of Jerusalem celebrated their decision to obey the laws of God.

 ## discussion questions

1. How many copies of God's law did the people of Judah have?
2. How many Bibles do you have at your house?

King Josiah's Hat

What you need

- crayons or markers

What you do

1. Photocopy this page for each child and cut out the image below. Leave space for children to add a crown.

2. Say, **Josiah was only eight years old when he became king. What hat did King Josiah wear when he became king?**

3. Children draw a crown on Josiah's head and color the rest of the picture.

Top 50 Creative Bible Lessons: Fun Activities for Preschoolers

Bookmark for God's Word

What you need

- scissors or papercutter
- crayons or markers
- glue
- 9-inch piece of yarn or ribbon, one for each child

What you do

1. Photocopy the crowns and Bibles below, making one set for each child. Cut out the squares. Older children may be able to cut for themselves. They can choose to cut out the squares, or use the cutting lines to cut around the shapes.
2. Children color the crowns and the Bibles.
3. Children glue one end of a length of yarn between the two crowns and the other end between the two Bibles to make two bookmarks. Keep one for your Bible and give one to a friend.

Bible Patterns

What you need

• crayons or markers

What you do

1. Photocopy this page for each child.

2. Children look at each row of Bibles and decide which one is different and cross it out.

3. Answers: Row 1 = second Bible; Row 2 = third Bible; Row 3 = first Bible

Josiah Respects God's Word

The New King (based on 2 Chronicles 34:8–33)

memory verse

Don't just listen to God's word. You must do what it says. James 1:22

discussion questions

1. How many copies of God's law did the people of Judah have?

2. How many Bibles do you have at your house?

God's Word Is Found

Long ago God's word was written on tablets of stone or scrolls. Draw a line between the pictures that match.

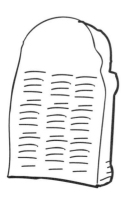

Daniel and the Lions

memory verse

Love the LORD your God and always obey his . . . commands. Deuteronomy 11:1

Daniel Prays Only to God (based on Daniel 6)

Daniel was a man who loved and obeyed God. When he was a teenager, Daniel and other young people were taken from their home to a foreign land. Once there, Daniel always worked to obey God, no matter what.

The king of this land, King Darius, had grown to respect Daniel's wisdom. King Darius put Daniel in charge of the kingdom. But there were men who didn't want Daniel to rule over them! So they planned to make the king angry with Daniel.

"King Darius," they said. "You are so wonderful. Nobody should pray to anyone but you. If anyone breaks that rule, they should be thrown to the lions."

King Darius thought that was a great idea. But Daniel still prayed to God—and only to God—three times a day. When the men saw Daniel praying, they went to the king. "Daniel is breaking your rule!" they said.

The king was sorry he had made the rule. He loved Daniel. Now he had to throw Daniel to the lions.

Early the next morning, the king rushed to the lions' den. "Daniel," he called. "Has your God rescued you from the lions?"

"Yes!" Daniel said. "My God sent an angel to shut the lions' mouths."

King Darius was very happy. He had his men take Daniel out of the lions' den. Then the king told all the people that God took care of Daniel.

discussion questions

1. Where did the king put Daniel when he broke the rule?
2. Why didn't the lions hurt Daniel?

Daniel Story Path

What you need

- scissors or papercutter
- crayons or markers

What you do

1. Photocopy this page and cut out activity. Older children may be able to cut for themselves.

2. Children color pictures and follow path as you briefly retell the Bible story.

What to Say

Daniel was a very good man. He prayed to God every day (Picture 1).

The king made a rule that whoever prayed to God would be put in a den with hungry lions (Picture 2).

Daniel was not afraid. He still prayed to God (Picture 3).

The king was very sad (Picture 4), but he had Daniel put in the lions' den.

God kept Daniel safe. God closed the mouths of the lions so they did not hurt Daniel (Picture 5).

The king was very happy that God had taken care of Daniel (Picture 6).

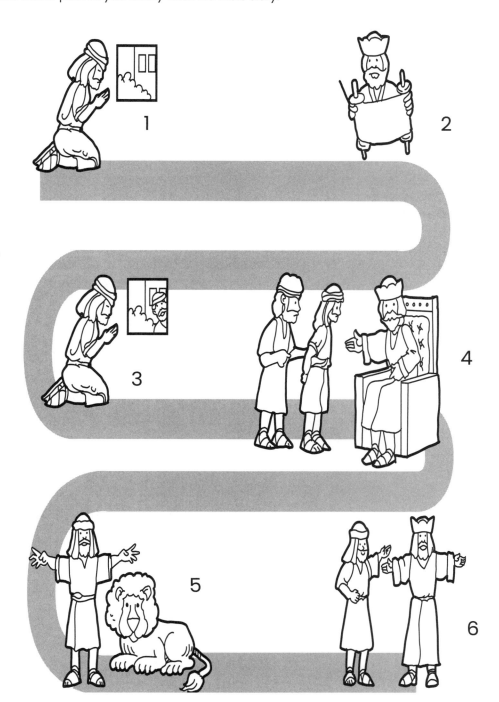

Lion Puppet

What you need

- scissors
- crayons or markers
- paper bag, one for each child
- glue

What you do

1. For each child, photocopy this page and cut out lion head and lower mouth pieces. Older children may be able to cut for themselves.
2. Children color the lion head and lower mouth pieces.
3. Children glue lion head to the bottom of a paper bag, as shown in the finished craft sketch below.
4. Children then glue the lower mouth piece where the bottom of the bag meets the side of the bag, as shown in the finished craft sketch below.

What to Say

Open the lion's mouth and make him ROAR! Now shut the puppet's mouth, just like God shut the real lions' mouths so that they could not hurt Daniel

finished craft

 Top 50 Creative Bible Lessons: Fun Activities for Preschoolers

Daniel Finger Play

What you need

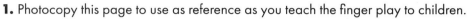

• none

What you do

1. Photocopy this page to use as reference as you teach the finger play to children.
2. Demonstrate the fun finger play below to help the children remember the Bible story of how God saved Daniel from the lions' den.
3. Children perform the finger play with you as time and interest allow.

The Lions

Lions growled,

Lions growled,

Lions growled,

But they could not bite.

 growl

 bite

Angel stayed close,

Angel stayed close,

Angel stayed close,

So lions could not bite.

 *cross arms on chest*

 bite

Daniel prayed,

Daniel prayed,

Daniel prayed,

And the lions did not bite.

 make praying hands

 bite

Daniel Prayed

Daniel prayed to God.

Daniel prayed to God.

Daniel prayed to God,

Not to the king.

 make praying hands

In the lions' den.

In the lions' den.

In the lions' den.

Daniel was thrown.

 make a scared face

An angel shut the lions' mouths.

An angel shut the lions' mouths.

An angel shut the lions' mouths.

And Daniel was saved.

 touch mouth with hand

The king believed in God.

The king believed in God.

The king believed in God.

All the people believed, too.

 point to God

Daniel and the Lions

Daniel Prays Only to God (based on Daniel 6)

memory verse

Love the LORD your God and always obey his . . . commands. Deuteronomy 11:1

discussion questions

1. Where did the king put Daniel when he broke the rule?

2. Why didn't the lions hurt Daniel?

God Protects Daniel

Daniel loved God and always did his best to please God. When some bad men wanted to kill Daniel by putting him in a den with hungry lions, God protected Daniel from the lions and they did not hurt him.

Color the picture. If you have some yellow yarn, you can glue it to the lion's mane.

 Top 50 Creative Bible Lessons: Fun Activities for Preschoolers

Esther Prays to God

memory verse

Don't worry about anything; instead, pray about everything. Philippians 4:6

Esther Helps Her People (based on Esther)

Once upon a time in Persia, there was a king who was looking for a queen. King Xerxes was searching for a beautiful, young girl to marry. So his people were instructed to find the most beautiful girls in the kingdom and bring them to the palace so that he could choose one to be his queen. One of ladies chosen was named Esther.

Esther was very pretty. Esther had no parents, so her cousin Mordecai had been taking care of her as if she were his own daughter. Mordecai worked for King Xerxes.

Mordecai and Esther were Jewish. Their family was one of many families that had been taken away from Israel many years earlier. Modecai cautioned Esther not to tell anyone that she was Jewish. There were some people in Persia who didn't like the Jewish people.

One day, the girls were taken into the king's palace and given beauty treatments before they were presented to the king. When the girls were presented to the king, he chose beautiful Esther, not knowing that she was a Jew.

Haman was a very bad man who talked the king into making a law that allowed Jews to be killed on a certain day. Mordecai told Queen Esther about the law and begged her to talk to the king to stop it. The problem was, the law said that even the queen couldn't talk to the king without his permission!

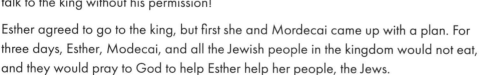

Esther agreed to go to the king, but first she and Mordecai came up with a plan. For three days, Esther, Modecai, and all the Jewish people in the kingdom would not eat, and they would pray to God to help Esther help her people, the Jews.

Esther was a brave woman. After the three days of prayer were over, she asked the king to save her and all the Jews. The king listened to Esther, and he stopped Haman's evil plan to kill the Jews. Esther helped save God's people.

discussion questions

1. What group of people was Haman trying to kill?
2. Who did Esther ask for help before going to see King Xerxes?

Royal Robes

What you need

- scissors or papercutter
- crayons or markers

What you do

1. Photocopy this page and cut out activity. Older children may be able to cut for themselves.

2. Children color pictures and draw a line from Esther to the things she might have worn to visit the king.

What to Say

The king needed a new queen. He picked Esther. Esther was beautiful. The king gave her beautiful clothes and jewelry. She was a successful queen because she prayed to God for help when she needed it. We can pray to God for help, too. God always hears our prayers.

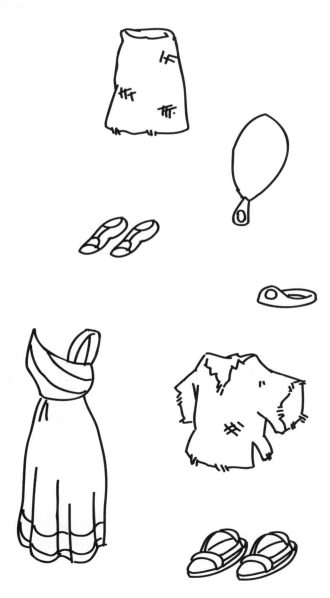

Esther Story Crown

What you need

- white card stock
- scissors
- crayons or markers
- gem stickers

What you do

1. On card stock, photocopy this page and cut out crowns. Older children may be able to cut for themselves. Prefold on dashed line to make a book.

2. Children color both sides of their crowns and then place gem stickers on the crowns.

3. Children open books and follow along (or look at pictures) as you read the book to them.

What to Say

While Esther was queen, she heard there was a wicked plot against her people. Esther wanted to tell the king about this plot, but she wasn't supposed to go to the king if he didn't invite her. Esther prayed for God to help her. The king agreed to see Esther. When she told him about the evil plans, he stopped them. Esther had saved the Jews.

Esther prayed for God's great help.
She bravely told the king.

I can pray for God's help, too,
And then my heart will sing!

Crown Toss Game

What you need

- brightly colored card stock
- scissors
- 24-ounce soda or juice bottle with lid
- uncooked rice or beans, dry
- construction paper
- crayons or markers
- tape

What you do

1. On card stock, make three or more photocopys of the crown on this page, enlarging crown to 150%.
2. Cut out crowns, including the inner circle.
3. Fill the soda bottle with an inch or two of rice or beans. Place the lid tightly on the bottle.
4. Cut a piece of construction paper as tall as the soda or juice bottle and wide enough to go around the bottle. Draw a "Queen Esther" on the construction paper and tape around the bottle.
5. To play the game, children stand a few feet away from the "Queen Esther" bottle and toss a crown to get it over the bottle. Praise children for their efforts, even if they don't get the crown onto the bottle.
6. Let younger children stand right over the bottle to try to drop the crown onto the bottle.

What to Say

Queen Esther wore a crown. Let's try to toss the crowns on the queen's head.

Queen Esther was brave because she prayed to God for help. We can pray to God, too!

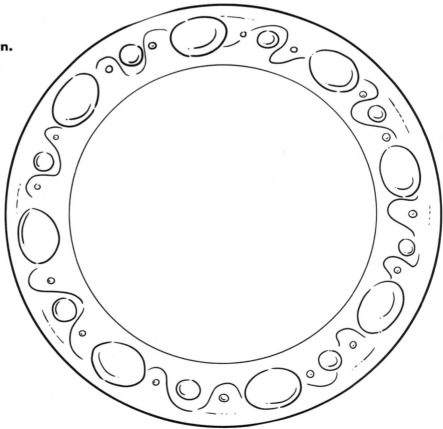

Esther Prays to God

Esther Helps Her People (based on Esther)

memory verse

Don't worry about anything; instead, pray about everything. Philippians 4:6

discussion questions

1. What group of people was Haman trying to kill?

2. Who did Esther ask for help before going to see King Xerxes?

God Helps Esther Be Brave

Color the picture of Queen Esther and King Xerxes. Use glitter glue to decorate the king's and queen's crowns and jewelry.

"Don't worry about anything; instead, pray about everything."
Philippians 4:6

Nehemiah Is Fair

memory verse

Remember, the Lord forgave you, so you must forgive others. Colossians 3:13

Give It Back! (based on Nehemiah 5:1–19)

There was trouble in Jerusalem! The people were busy rebuilding the walls of Jerusalem under the leadership of Nehemiah. This was good, but the people were treating each other badly.

The rich men were being mean to the poor. There was no food in Jerusalem because their enemies were able to get through the broken walls and steal all their crops. The poor were desperate for food.

"I'll give you food," said one rich man. "But you must give me your land if you can't pay."

When the poor couldn't pay the rich what they owed them, they forced the poor man's sons and daughters to become their slaves. The rich took their vineyards and lands so the poor couldn't work to get their families back.

"Help us, Nehemiah," they cried.

Nehemiah was angry. "What you are doing is not good," he told the rich men. "It is not fair for you to take the land and vineyards that belong to others. You should give back the houses, land, and money."

The rich hung their heads. "Yes, Nehemiah, we will obey. We will give back what belongs to them."

Nehemiah called the priest. "Give the priest a promise that you will do what you have said."

Then Nehemiah shook his robe. "May God shake each of you out of your homes and lands who doesn't keep his promise, just as I shook out my robe."

"Amen!" God's people said. "We have learned to be fair. Praise the Lord."

discussion questions

1. Who was unfair in our story?
2. Who told them what they were doing was wrong?

A Handy Holder

What you need

- cardstock
- scissors
- yarn
- crayons or markers
- glue
- spring-type clothespins
- magnet strips
- scrap paper

What you do

1. On card stock, photocopy and cut out a hand for each child. Cut the yarn into 7-inch pieces, one for each child.
2. Children color the hands.
3. Show how to glue a clothespin on the hand and the magnet to the back.
4. Help the children tie a yarn bow around the first finger.
5. Show how to clip several pieces of paper with the holder.

What to Say

Sometimes, when people want to remember something, they tie a string around a finger. We want to remember our memory verses. Every time you see this memo holder remember "The Lord forgave you, so you must forgive others" (Colossians 3:13).

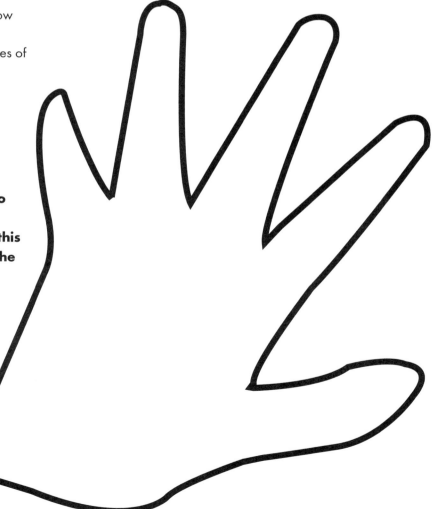

Help the Builders

What you need

- scissors or papercutter
- crayons or markers

What you do

1. Photocopy the picture for each child and cut out. Older children may be able to cut for themselves.

2. Children help the builders finish the wall by drawing it.

3. Children color the picture.

Fair Games

What you need

- scissors or papercutter
- crayons or markers

What you do

1. Photocopy the page for each child and cut out matching activity. Older children may be able to cut for themselves.

2. Say, **When you play games you need to play fair. Cheating does not make God happy. Many times, others may not play as well as you. Remember, "The Lord forgave you, so you must forgive others" (Colossians 3:13).**

3. Children match the pictures of games by drawing lines between them.

Nehemiah Is Fair

Give It Back! (based on Nehemiah 5:1–19)

memory verse

Remember, the Lord forgave you, so you must forgive others. Colossians 3:13

discussion questions

1. Who was unfair in our story?

2. Who told them what they were doing was wrong?

Unhappy Builders

The people who were rebuilding the walls of Jerusalem were not happy because of the way the rich were treating them. When Nehemiah encouraged the rich men to be fair, the poor people's frowns turned upside-down. Color the picture and then put happy face stickers over the sad faces.

God Promises a Child

memory verse

Praise be to the Lord. Luke 1:68

An Angel Appears to Zechariah (based on Luke 1:5–25; 57–80)

Zechariah and Elizabeth were very old, but they didn't have any children. They really wanted to have a child.

One day when Zechariah was working in the temple, an angel appeared. He said, "You and your wife are going to have a son. Name him *John*."

Zechariah couldn't believe his ears. "A baby? I'm too old!" he said. But the angel said the baby would bring joy to many people. Zechariah still couldn't believe that he and Elizabeth would have a baby. The angel said, "I have been sent by God to tell you this good news. Because you do not believe me, you will not be able to talk until the baby is born."

Elizabeth had a baby boy, just like the angel said. Everyone was very happy that Elizabeth and Zechariah finally had a child of their own. "Name him after his father," some of the people said.

But Zechariah, who still couldn't talk, wrote on a tablet, "His name is John." Immediately, Zechariah could talk again! Zechariah, Elizabeth, and John were a happy family.

 discussion questions

1. What did Zechariah and Elizabeth want?
2. What did they name their baby boy?
3. What is something you want to praise God for?

Zechariah Speaks

What you need

- scissors or papercutter
- crayons or markers

What you do

1. Photocopy this page and cut out activity. Older children may be able to cut for themselves.

2. On the blanks below each picture, children write the first letter of the object in the picture.

3. Children color pictures.

What to Say

Zechariah could not speak until the day his son was born. Write the first letter of each word to find the name of the baby.

_____   _____   _____   _____

Story Puppets

What you need

- scissors or papercutter
- crayons or markers
- craft sticks, 4 for each child
- tape

What you do

1. Photocopy this page and cut out the four puppets. Older children may be able to cut for themselves.
2. Children color the puppets.
3. Tape a craft stick to the bottom edge of each puppet.
4. Children use the puppets as you briefly tell the story.

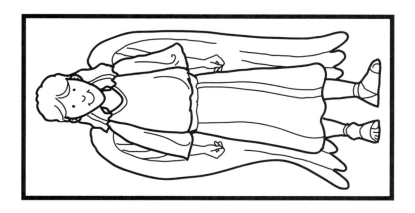

Family Songs

What you need

- none

What you do

1. Photocopy this page to use as reference as you teach the song and finger play to children.
2. Sing "Praise" with the children to the tune of "The Farmer in the Dell." Add actions by pointing up when you say "Lord" in each line.
3. Say the "My Family" finger play using the motions shown. Do rhyme with the children a few times as they learn the motions.

My Family

Daddy  *stand tall*

Mommy  *crouch a little shorter*

Sister
(or brother, pet, cousin, etc.)  *crouch a little shorter*

And me *crouch a little shorter*

We are all a family!  *stand up and spread arms wide*

Praise be to the Lord.
Praise be to the Lord.
He gave John a family.
Praise be to the Lord.

Praise be to the Lord
Praise be to the Lord
He gave me a family,
Praise be to the Lord.

God Promises a Child

An Angel Appears to Zechariah (based on Luke 1:5–25; 57–80)

memory verse

Praise the Lord. Luke 1:68

discussion questions

1. What did Zechariah and Elizabeth want?

2. What did they name their baby boy?

3. What is something you want to praise God for?

Puzzle Story

Color the puzzle and cut it out. After reading the story aloud, put the puzzle pieces together.

Zechariah and Elizabeth wanted to have a family. But, they were very old. One day an angel appeared to Zechariah in the temple.

"You and your wife will have a baby boy," the angel said. "His name will be John. He will be great among his people."

But Zechariah just couldn't believe this was true. He and Elizabeth were too old to have a baby! The angel told Zechariah, "Since you don't believe the Lord's word, you will not speak until after the baby is born."

Zechariah left the temple and wasn't able to talk.

Soon, Elizabeth had a baby. Elizabeth and Zechariah were very happy. They named the baby *John*.

(Luke 1:5–25, 57–80)

Jesus Is God's Son

memory verse

[God said,] "This is my dearly loved Son." Mark 9:7

No Room at the Inn (based on Luke 1:26–38; 2:1–7)

One day an angel appeared to Mary. The angel said, "Mary, you will have a son. You are to give him the name *Jesus*. He will be the Son of God."

Mary and Joseph had to travel to Bethlehem. People everywhere traveled to their hometown to register their names. It was a long trip. Mary's baby would be born any time.

When they arrived in Bethlehem, Joseph looked for a place for them to stay. There was no room at the inn, so they stayed in the stable. Mary's baby was born. She wrapped him in cloths and placed him in a manger. Mary gave the baby the name the angel told her to give him. The baby was named Jesus. Jesus is God's Son.

 discussion questions
1. What did the angel tell Mary?
2. Where was Jesus born?

Shepherds and Angel Ornament

What you need

- scissors
- tape
- crayons or markers
- yarn

What you do

1. Photocopy and cut out both star shapes for each child. Older children may be able to cut for themselves.
2. Help the children match the star shapes and tape them together with the printed sides facing out.
3. Children color the stars.
4. Tape a loop of yarn to the top point of the star.
5. Read the memory verse on one side of the star to the children.

What to Say

After Jesus was born, God sent angels to tell others the Good News!

[God said,] "This is my dearly loved Son."
Mark 9:7

Hidden Picture Puzzle

What you need

- scissors or papercutter
- crayons or markers

What you do

1. For each child, photocopy this page and cut out activity. Older children may be able to cut for themselves.

2. Help the children find the hidden animals in the stable.

3. Children color the animals they find. (There are four.)

4. Encourage children to name each animal they find.

What to Say

Mary wrapped her baby in cloths and placed him in a manger. his name is Jesus. Jesus is God's Son.

[God said,] "This is my dearly loved Son."

Mark 9:7

A Blanket for Jesus

What you need

- scissors
- flannel
- ruler
- crayons or markers
- letter envelope, one for each child
- yellow paper

What you do

1. For each child, photocopy this page and cut out baby Jesus figure. Older children may be able to cut for themselves.
2. Cut an 8×8-inch square of flannel for each child.
3. Children color their baby Jesus figure. Children also color an envelope as the manger.
4. Give each child a square of flannel and show them how to wrap baby Jesus. (See images below.)
5. Children cut strips of yellow paper and place inside the envelope manger. They then place their wrapped baby Jesus in the manger.

Tip: For younger children, cut strips of yellow paper.

Mary took good care of baby Jesus. When you take home your baby Jesus and his manger, you can tell your family about Jesus being born in a manger and how Mary and Joseph took good care of him.

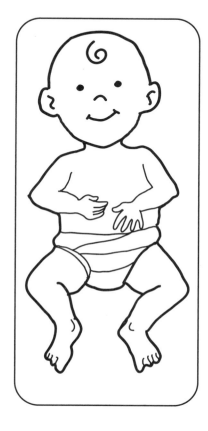

place flannel square this way

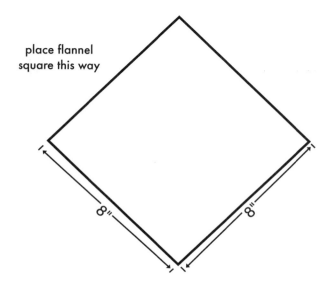

8" 8"

fold flannel as shown

Top 50 Creative Bible Lessons: Fun Activities for Preschoolers.

Jesus Is God's Son

No Room at the Inn (based on Luke 1:26–38; 2:1–7)

memory verse

[God said,] "This is my dearly loved Son." Mark 9:7

discussion questions

1. What did the angel tell Mary?

2. Where was Jesus born?

A Special Night

How many things can you find wrong in this picture? Circle the wrong things and color the picture.

The Wise Men

memory verse

God loves a a person who gives cheerfully. 2 Corinthians 9:7

Gifts for Jesus (based on Matthew 2:1–14)

"Laben," said one of the wise men, looking up at the stars. "Laben, come quickly. There's a new star in the sky."

Laben hurried over to where his friends Simon and David were looking toward Heaven. "Where, what kind of star?"

David pointed. "There, it's the brightest star I've ever seen," he said quietly.

The wise men stared at the star. It WAS the brightest star they had ever seen. It was telling them that a king had been born. Without delay, the wise men prepared for the journey. They would take gifts to this new king and worship him.

The men traveled for long days. They grew tired and eager to reach their destination. Over and over they talked about the king of the Jews— the tiny baby whose star they had seen.

One day, Mary heard loud noises. Rushing to the window, she gasped in surprise. Camels? And who were these men riding them? They looked like important men, at least rich men. Their robes were colorful and made of the finest fabrics.

Mary watched in amazement as the men asked permission to see the baby, the king of the Jews. Tears filled her eyes as each of these important guests bowed on their knees and worshiped her son.

Simon handed Joseph a gift. "This is my gift to the baby Jesus. It is gold to show he is King."

Laben handed Joseph his gift. "My gift is frankincense. This incense is burned to make the air sweet in honor of God. Somehow this baby is both man and God."

Bowing his head, David offered his gift. "My gift is myrrh, a special perfume worn only by important men. It is also used to prepare them for burial." Somehow David knew this God who had become man would die.

Mary and Joseph tried to thank the wise men for their gifts. "You have given your gifts so willingly. May you be blessed."

Bowing low, the wise men once again worshiped Jesus.

discussion questions
1. What would you give as a gift to baby Jesus?
2. What should your face look like when you give?

A Gift for Jesus

What you need

- scissors or papercutter
- crayons or markers

What you do

1. For each child, photocopy this page and cut out dot-to-dot activity. Older children may be able to cut for themselves.

2. Say, **Follow the dots to see what gift you can give to Jesus.**

3. Children color the heart.

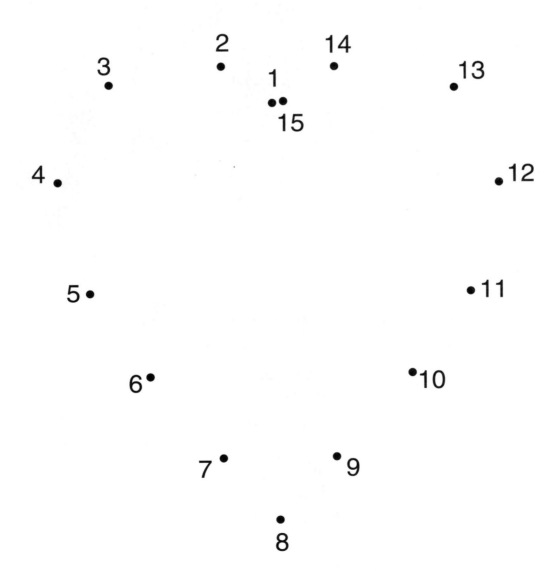

"God loves a person who gives cheerfully."

2 Corinthians 9:7

What Is Inside?

What you need

- scissors or papercutter
- crayons or markers

What you do

1. For each child, photocopy this page and cut out shape-matching activity. Older children may be able to cut for themselves.
2. Children draw lines to match the gifts on the left with the outlines of them around the wise men's gifts on the right.
3. Children color the pictures.

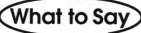

What to Say

The wise men gave gifts to Jesus. You can give Jesus your heart.

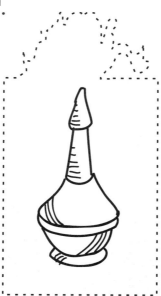

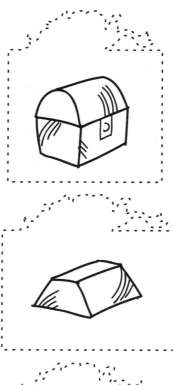

Cheerful Givers

What you need

- scissors or papercutter
- crayons or markers

What you do

1. Photocopy this page and cut out activity. Older children may be able to cut for themselves.

2. Children look at the objects in the circles, and find the objects in the big picture, drawing a line between each circle and where the object is hidden. (Note: The objects do not look the same in each drawing. This is an activity to recognize objects when they look different.)

What to Say

Some very wise men left their homes and traveled very far to find the new king. Where did the star took them? (To Bethlehem) **The wise men brought wonderful gifts for the baby king. They were happy to show Jesus their love. What "gifts" could you give Jesus?** (Love, helping others, obeying parents, etc.)

The Wise Men

Gifts for Jesus (based on Matthew 2:1–14))

memory verse

God loves a person who gives cheerfully. 2 Corinthians 9:7

discussion questions

1. What would you give as a gift to baby Jesus?

2. What should your face look like when you give?

Wise Men Visit baby Jesus

Color the picture of the wise men's visit to baby Jesus.

Jesus at the Temple

memory verse

Jesus grew in wisdom. Luke 2:52

Growing in Wisdom (based on Luke 2:41–52)

Mary and Joseph went to Jerusalem to celebrate Passover and other special holidays. Jesus and his family went to Jerusalem every year. Traveling to Jerusalem from Nazareth, their hometown, took three whole days. The roads were dangerous because robbers were around, so people traveled in big groups.

The group was headed back to Nazareth when Joseph and Mary made a terrible discovery.

Jesus was missing! He was not with the other children in the group. He wasn't anywhere!

Mary and Joseph searched everywhere! Finally, they knew there was only one place he could be: back in Jerusalem.

Mary and Joseph made the long journey back to Jerusalem. Three days later, they found Jesus in the temple. There he was, talking to the temple leaders. Jesus asked them hard questions. They were amazed that a 12-year-old could ask such questions.

"Son, how could you worry us like this?" Mary asked.

"Why did you search around for me?" Jesus asked. "Didn't you know I would be in my Father's house?" Mary and Joseph did not understand what he meant.

Jesus returned home to Nazareth with them and was an obedient son. Every day, Jesus grew in wisdom and in God's favor.

discussion questions

1. Why were Mary and Joseph worried?
2. Where was Jesus? What was he doing?
3. How do your parents show their concern for you?

CHAPTER

25

Going to Jerusalem

What you need

- scissors or papercutter
- crayons or markers

What to do

1. Photocopy this page and cut out activity. Older children may be able to cut for themselves.

2. Children circle the items that they think Jesus would have taken on his trip to Jerusalem.

What to Say

Jesus traveled to Jerusalem with his parents for Passover. When it was time for Jesus and his family to go home, Jesus stayed behind to continue learning from the teachers. He wanted to grow in wisdom. Listening to Bible stories is a good way for you to grow in knowledge and wisdom, too. What are the kinds of things you might take on a trip?

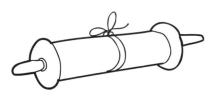

God's House Book

What you need

- crayons or markers

What to do

1. For each child, photocopy page 129. Make a sample craft to show the children.

2. Show the children the sample craft and distribute a pattern page to each child.

3. Demonstrate how to accordion-fold the page on the dashed lines (see sketch below). Assist children as they fold their pages.

4. Children trace the picture of God's House in the center section. The children may color the page as they want.

What to Say

Jesus loved going to God's house and talking with others about God. I'm so glad that we get to go to God's house, too! What do you like to do best in God's house? (Children respond.) What do you think Jesus liked to do in God's house? (Children respond.)

One thing we know Jesus like to do was study God's Word. We study God's Word, too! The Bible says, "Jesus grew in wisdom." When we go to God's house and talk with others about God, we're growing in wisdom, too. Just like Jesus!

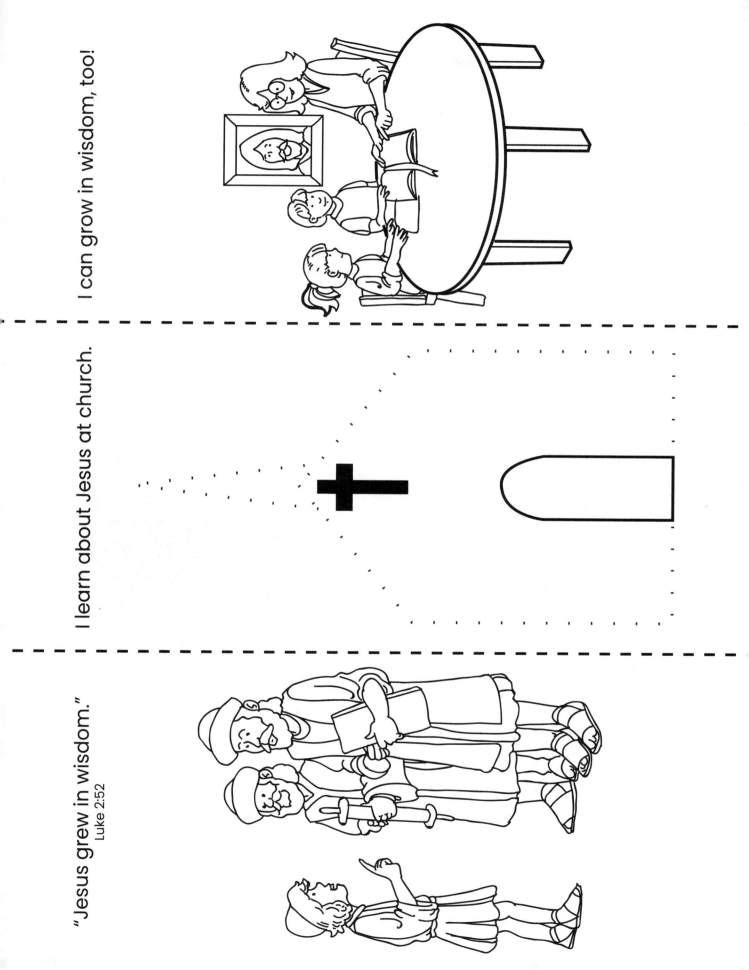

I can grow in wisdom, too!

I learn about Jesus at church.

"Jesus grew in wisdom."
Luke 2:52

How Many?

What you need

- crayons or markers

What you do

1. Photocopy this page for each child and cut out activity. Older children may be able to cut for themselves.

2. Say, **Mary and Joseph asked many people if they had seen their son, Jesus. Count the people in each picture and write the number in the square.**

3. Children color the pictures.

 Top 50 Creative Bible Lessons: Fun Activities for Preschoolers

Jesus at the Temple

Growing in Wisdom (based on Luke 2:41–52)

memory verse

Jesus grew in wisdom. Luke 2:52

discussion questions

1. Why were Mary and Joseph worried?

2. Where was Jesus? What was he doing?

3. How do members of your family show concern for each other?

Jesus Helps His Family

Look at the picture with a 1 in the box. Jesus is just starting a new day. Put the rest of his day in order. Put a number in the empty square in each of the other pictures: 2, 3, 4, and 5. Number 2 will be what you think happens next. Then number 3. After that number 4. Number 5 will be what you think happens last.

John Baptizes Jesus

memory verse

*How beautiful are the feet of messengers
who bring good news!* Romans 10:15

Talking about Jesus (based on Matthew 3:1–17)

John the Baptist wandered from place to place, telling people about God and how much God loves us. John the Baptist was Jesus' cousin. God had given John a very important message.

As crowds sat on the river bank listening to him preach, John said, "What I have to tell you is that you need to get ready. Get ready for the one who is coming soon. Turn from your sin. The Kingdom of Heaven will soon be here."

John's words were different from what the people had heard before. Everything about John was different. He wore clothes that were roughly woven from camel's hair and held together with a leather belt. He ate dried grasshoppers dipped in wild honey he found in the trees. Many thought he was strange, but many believed and stopped doing wrong things.

"Stop sinning, doing wrong things," John preached. And as people obeyed, John baptized them in the Jordan River.

"I'm baptizing you with water," said John, "but this king who comes after me is so good and pure, I am not even worthy to unfasten his sandals."

One day while John was baptizing those who had decided to follow God's way, John looked up to see Jesus waiting to be baptized. This was the one he had been preaching about. This was the king he had said was coming! "I can't baptize you, Jesus," said John. "You are too pure and good."

Jesus said, "My Father, God, wants us all to be baptized to show that we believe in him."

John obeyed Jesus and baptized him in the Jordan River. When he did, the voice of God could be heard. "This is my Son, and I love him," said God. "He pleases me."

John continued telling others the good news of Jesus.

 ## discussion questions
1. Who first told you about Jesus? You can thank them for sharing the good news about Jesus.
2. What do you want to tell others about Jesus?

Baptism Puzzle

What you need

- scissors
- crayons or markers

What to do

1. For each child, photocopy this page and cut out puzzle pieces and puzzle board. Do not cut individual puzzle pieces. Older children may be able to cut for themselves.

2. Children color and then cut out the puzzle pieces.

3. Children put the puzzle pieces together on the puzzle board.

What to Say

Jesus had a cousin who loved God. His name was John. He was called John the Baptist because he told people about God and baptized them. Jesus wanted to teach people that baptism was a good way to show people that they were following God's rules. So Jesus asked John to baptize him, too.

Everywhere he went, John told others about Jesus. You can be like John and tell others about Jesus, too.

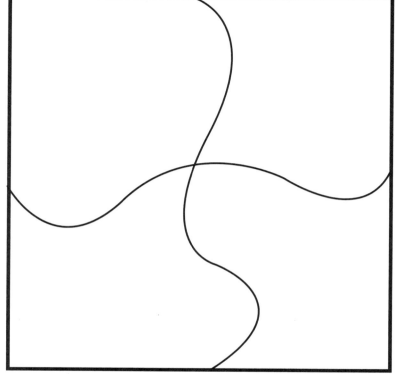

John's Clothes

What you need

- scissors
- instant coffee grains
- 9×13-inch pan
- glue
- shallow bowls
- paint brushes

Optional

- transparent tape

What to do

1. Photocopy and cut out John and clothes, one set per child. Older children may be able to cut for themselves.
2. Pour the coffee grounds in the pan. Pour glue into shallow bowls. Set bowls and paint brushes on tables for children to use.
3. Children brush glue on John's coat.
4. Children lay the coat in the coffee, glue side down, and shake off excess coffee.
5. Children place the coat on John and fold the tabs back.

Optional: Tape the coat securely onto each child's John figure.

What to Say

What you wear isn't important to Jesus. John wore a coat of camel's hair. But he pleased Jesus by telling others about him. Jesus will be pleased with you if you use your feet to go tell your friends about him.

Shoe Match

What you need

- scissors or papercutter
- crayons or markers

What to do

1. Photocopy the page and cut out activity for each child. Older children may be able to cut for themselves

2. Children draw a line from the small shoe to the large one that matches it.

3. Children color the shoes.

What to Say

Just like each pair of shoes is different, all of you are different, too. You will all tell others about Jesus in your own special way.

John Baptizes Jesus

Talking about Jesus (based on Matthew 3:1–17)

memory verse

How beautiful are the feet of those who bring good news! Romans 10:15

discussion questions

1. Who first told you about Jesus? You can say thank you to them for sharing the good news about Jesus.

2. What do you want to tell others about Jesus?

Baptism Book

God was pleased when Jesus asked John to baptize him. Here is a storybook about Jesus' baptism. Color the pictures. Then cut out on the solid lines and fold on the dashed lines.

God said, "I love you, Son. You make me happy."

Jesus asked his cousin John to baptize him.

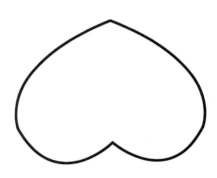

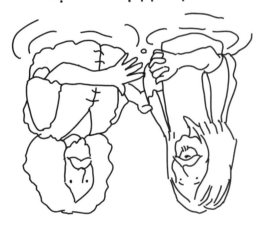

Everywhere he went, John told people the good news about Jesus

Jesus Is Baptized

Matthew 3:1–17

Jesus Calls Helpers

memory verse

Jesus called out to them, "Come, follow me." Mark 1:17

Fishers of Men (based on Mark 1:16–20; 2:13–17; 3:13–19)

Jesus needed some helpers. He needed people who would follow him wherever he went and help him teach people about God and Heaven.

Jesus walked beside the Sea of Galilee. There he saw Simon Peter and his brother Andrew throwing a fish net into the lake. They were fishermen.

Jesus said to Peter and Andrew, "Come, follow me. I will make you fishers of men." Peter and Andrew left their fishing nets and followed Jesus.

Later, Jesus saw James and his brother John fixing their fishing nets in a boat. Jesus called them to be his helpers, too.

Another day, Jesus saw Matthew collecting taxes. "Follow me," Jesus said. Matthew left his tax table.

All together, Jesus called twelve people to be his helpers. Their names were: Peter, Andrew, James, John, Philip, Bartholomew, Matthew, Thomas, James, Thaddaeus, Simon, and Judas.

 discussion questions

1. What were Peter, Andrew, James, and John doing before Jesus called them?
2. What did Jesus tell Peter and Andrew they would become?
3. How many people did Jesus call to be his helpers?

Follow Jesus Plaque

What you need

- scissors or papercutter
- hole punch
- shoebox lid, one for each child
- crayons or markers
- glue
- rickrack or other trim
- 12-inch lengths of yarn
- tape

What you do

1. Photocopy this page and cut out the picture for each child. Older children may be able to cut for themselves.
2. Punch two holes at each end of the top rim of each shoebox lid.
3. Children color a picture of Jesus.
4. Help each child glue a picture of Jesus in the center of the shoebox lid.
5. Help children glue rickrack or other trim around the edge of the picture.
6. Children thread a length of yarn through the knots for hanging the picture. Tape yarn to secure.

finished craft

Happy Faces

What you need

- scissors or papercutter
- crayons or markers

What to do

1. For each child, photocopy this page and cut out the activity. Older children may be able to cut for themselves.
2. Children draw a happy smile on Jesus and each of his followers.
3. Children point to each person as you count all of the faces aloud.

What to Say

Jesus' helpers were named Peter, Andrew, James, John, Philip, Bartholomew, Matthew, Thomas, James, Thaddaeus, Simon, and Judas. Point to Jesus in the picture below. Now as we repeat the names of each follower, point to the man you think is the one we named.

Jesus called out to them, "Come, follow me."
Mark 1:17

Cereal Counting Fun

What you need

- scissors or papercutter
- crayons or markers
- round cereal pieces

What you do

1. Photocopy this page and cut out the game. Give each child a copy and twelve or more pieces of cereal.

2. Help the children count to twelve as they place their cereal pieces inside the circles on the page.

3. Count again. This time, each child will eat a piece of cereal for each number.

What to Say

Children say with you, **I will follow my friend Jesus.**

I will follow my friend Jesus!

1 2 3 4 5 6 7 8 9 10 11 12

Jesus Calls Helpers

Fishers of Men (based on Mark 1:16–20; 2:13–17; 3:13–19)

memory verse

Jesus called out to them, "Come, follow me." Mark 1:17

discussion questions

1. What were Peter, Andrew, James, and John doing before Jesus called them?

2. What did Jesus tell Peter and Andrew they would become?

3. How many people did Jesus call to be his helpers?

Fisherman of Fishermen

Look at the pictures in each row. Color the pictures in each row that look the same as the first picture in that row.

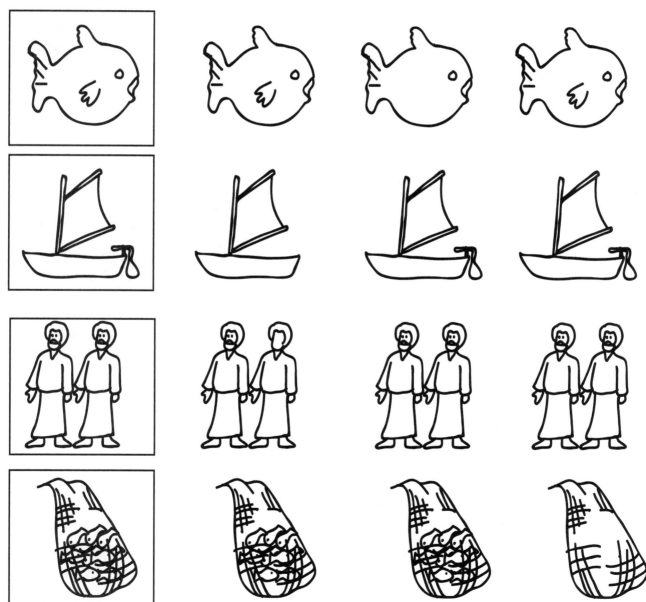

Jesus Makes People Well

memory verse

The touch of his hand healed every one. Luke 4:40

Healing Powers (based on Luke 4)

Jesus and his helpers traveled all around. Jesus taught people about God. He was God's Son.

Wherever Jesus went, people came to him to be healed. Sick people came to Jesus because they knew he could make them well. People with broken legs came to Jesus because they knew he could make them walk again.

Blind people came to Jesus because they knew he could make them see again.

Deaf people came to Jesus because they knew he could make them hear again.

One day, Jesus went to Peter's home. Peter's mother-in-law was sick. Jesus touched her and made her well.

People came to Jesus all day. Jesus touched the people, one by one, and made them well.

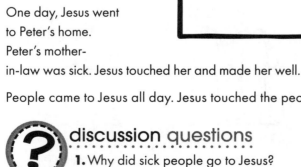 discussion questions

1. Why did sick people go to Jesus?
2. What did Jesus do when Peter's mother-in-law was sick?

Moving Picture

What you need

- scissors or papercutter
- crayons or markers
- hole punch
- brads (paper fasteners), one for each child

What you do

1. For each child, photocopy this page and cut out the scene and the Jesus figure. Older children may be able to cut for themselves.
2. Children color the scene and the Jesus figure.
3. Punch a hole and place a paper fastener through the hole in the Jesus figure and the indicated hole on the scene.
4. Retell the story. As you do, children tip forward the Jesus figure to show how Jesus touched many people to make them well.

Jesus Touched Them

What you need

- scissors
- hole punch
- crayons or markers
- yarn
- transparent tape

What you do

1. For each child, photocopy this page. Cut out Jesus figures and hands.
2. Punch a hole in each shoulder of the Jesus figure as indicated. Cut a 1-foot length of yarn for each child.
3. Children color the Jesus figure.
4. Help the children thread the yarn through the holes from the back.
5. Center and tape the yarn on the back of the figure.
6. Children tape a hand to each end of the yarn length.

What to Say

Children "touch" someone with Jesus' hands. **Jesus touched sick people and made them well.**

finished craft

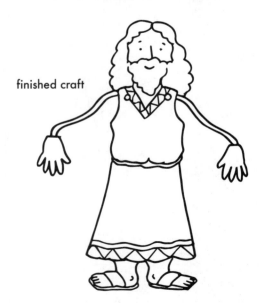

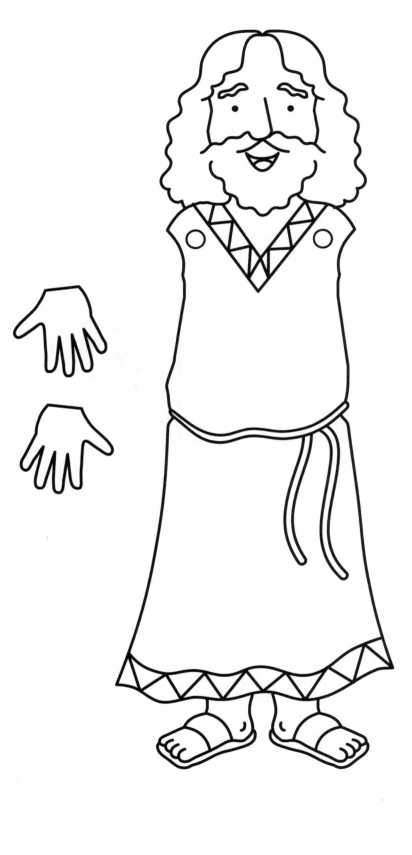

Song and Rhyme

What you need

- none

What to do

1. Photocopy this page to use as reference as you teach the song and finger play to children.

2. Sing "Jesus Made Many People Well" with the children to the tune of "Wheels on the Bus." As you lead the song, touch the head of each of the children.

3. Next, do the finger play. Slowly teach each action to the children so they will understand what to do.

What to Say

Jesus helped people by making them well. He helped blind people see, deaf people hear, and sick people well. This was one way Jesus showed God's love to others.

Jesus Made Many People Well

Jesus went around making people well,
People well,
People well.
Jesus went around making people well,
All through the town.

"Thank you, Jesus," the people said,
People said,
People said.
"Thank you, Jesus," the people said,
All through the town.

Jesus Touched

Touch, touch, touch.
Jesus touched a
blind man's eyes.

touch eyes

Touch, touch, touch.
Jesus touched a
deaf man's ears.

touch ears

Touch, touch, touch.
Jesus made sick
people well.

touch tummy

Jesus Makes People Well

Healing Powers (based on Luke 4)

memory verse

The touch of his hand healed every one. Luke 4:40

discussion questions

1. Why did sick people go to Jesus?

2. What did Jesus do when Peter's mother-in-law was sick?

Peter's Mother-in-Law

Peter and his mother-in-law lived a long time ago. They did not have many things that we have today. Look at the picture below. Circle the things that Peter's family would not have had in their home.

Parable of the Sower

memory verse

You must all be quick to listen, slow to speak, and slow to get angry. James 1:19

Can You Hear? (based on Matthew 13:3–23)

Jesus liked to tell stories. He knew stories helped people understand what he was trying to teach them. One day a crowd gathered to hear Jesus speak. This is the story he told:

> *Mr. Farmer was planting some seeds. Some of these seeds fell on the path beside the field. Caw, Caw, the birds called when they saw the seed. They swooped down and ate the seeds on the path.*
>
> *Other seeds fell on rocks. They tried to grow, but there wasn't water to give them the drinks they needed. These seeds died as soon as it became hot and they couldn't have a drink.*
>
> *Others of Mr. Farmer's seeds fell into the weeds and thistles. They, too, tried to grow, but the weeds were stronger than the tiny plants. They choked the plants until they died.*
>
> *But some seeds fell on good soil. They grew and grew, becoming strong and tall. Mr. Farmer was happy. He had a good crop from the seeds that fell on the good soil.*

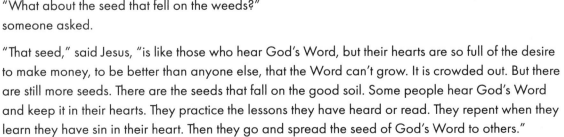

Jesus told the people, "The seeds in the story are like what you hear of God's Word. Just like the birds took the seeds from the path, the devil comes and steals what many hear from the Bible right out of their hearts. Others hear the Word, like those seeds which fell on the rocks, but when hard times come and things don't go their way, all they have heard is forgotten."

"What about the seed that fell on the weeds?" someone asked.

"That seed," said Jesus, "is like those who hear God's Word, but their hearts are so full of the desire to make money, to be better than anyone else, that the Word can't grow. It is crowded out. But there are still more seeds. There are the seeds that fall on the good soil. Some people hear God's Word and keep it in their hearts. They practice the lessons they have heard or read. They repent when they learn they have sin in their heart. Then they go and spread the seed of God's Word to others."

discussion questions

1. How can you show you are listening to the Bible?
2. How can you learn more about God's Word?

Listening Ears

What you need

- scissors or papercutter
- crayons or markers

What to do:

1. Photocopy this page and cut out activity. Older children may be able to cut for themselves.

2. Children compare the shadows with the animals and draw a line between the matching pairs.

What to Say

These animals all have ears. Our memory verse says, everyone should be "quick to listen." Is the verse talking about the animals? (Children respond.) **The animals and their interesting ears can remind us to be quick to listen.**

In the box, draw a picture of yourself as a reminder to be quick to listen.

Find the Seeds

What you need

- colored paper
- scissors
- card stock
- brown paper lunch bags
- stapler
- transparent tape

basket handle

What you do

1. On colored paper, photocopy the pictures of seeds several times and cut them out. Scatter the seeds around the room.
2. On card stock, photocopy and cut out a basket handle for each child.
3. Fold down the tops of the lunch bags three times. Give one to each child and assist in stapling the handles to the baskets. Cover the staples with tape to avoid injury.
4. Hold up a seed and say, **Mr. Farmer lost some seeds in our classroom. Let's see if you can find some seeds to put in your baskets. Each time you find a seed, say, "I am quick to listen."**
5. Monitor the children as they find the seeds. Help those who are having difficulty.

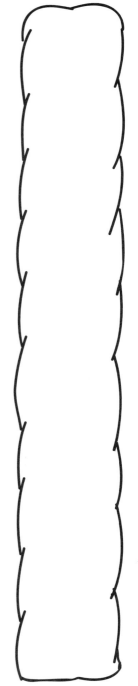

About Some Seeds

What you need

- scissors or papercutter
- crayons or markers

What to do

1. For each child, photocopy this page and cut out the activity.
Older children may be able to cut for themselves.

2. For each row, children color the number of objects shown at the beginning of the row.

What to Say

In today's story, Jesus said that the seed is the Word of God. Our hearts are the soil. If our hearts love God's Word and obey it, our hearts are like good soil.

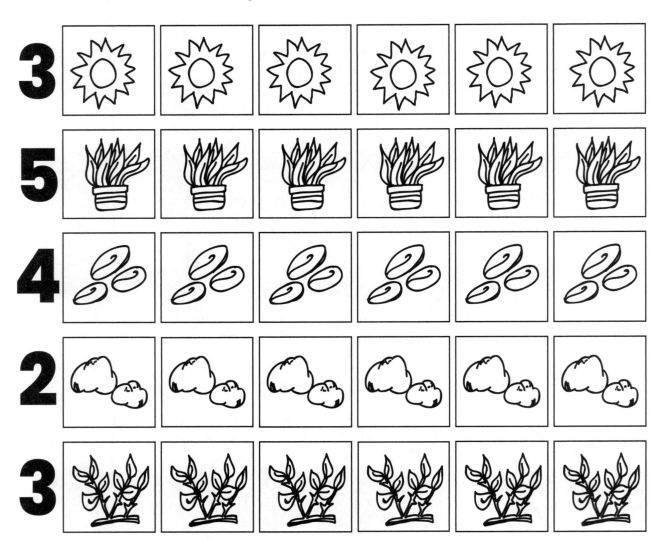

 Top 50 Creative Bible Lessons: Fun Activities for Preschoolers

Parable of the Sower

Can You Hear? (based on Matthew 13:3–23)

 memory verse

You must all be quick to listen, slow to speak, and slow to get angry. James 1:19

 discussion questions

1. How can you show you are listening to God's Word, the Bible?

2. How can you learn more about God's Word?

This Is The Way

Sing the song to the tune of "This Is the Way." Demonstrate the motions with children until they can do them with you.

This is the way we sow the seed,
Sow the seed, sow the seed.
This is the way we sow the seed,
Just like Mr. Farmer.

Pretend to put hands in bag and spread the seed

This is the ways we shoo the birds,
Shoo the birds, shoo the birds.
This is the way we shoo the birds,
Coming for dinner.

Shoo away the birds.

This is the way we listen to God,
Listen to God, listen to God.
This is the way we listen to God,
Listen to God's Word.

Cup your ears with your hands

Everyone here should be quick,
Should be quick, should be quick.
Everyone here should be quick,
To listen to God's Word.

Snap your fingers with each "quick"

Parable of the Great Banquet

memory verse

Respect everyone. 1 Peter 2:17

Come to the Party (based on Matthew 22:1–14)

Do you like to hear stories? Jesus knew that people like stories, so that's how he taught people. All his stories helped the people know how to live for God.

One day, Jesus told the story of a king who was preparing a big party. The party was in honor of his son's marriage. In Bible times, wedding receptions were large gatherings. If you were rich, you could invite the entire city to your party. A king's party lasted seven whole days, and the king expected his guests to stay until the end. For poor people who needed to work on their land, this was a hardship. But because they respected their king, they would attend the reception if they were invited.

In Jesus' story about a king and his party, the king invited many important people.

"Tell those I have invited that everything is ready," he told the men issuing the invitation.

But when the invitations were offered to the rich people, they made excuses.

"I can't come. I need to tend to my field," said one important person.

"I can't come either," said another rich person. "I have my business to run."

"Forget the important people," the king said when he heard the excuses. "Give the invitations to the poor people. Go anywhere you can to find them. They will show respect to my son and me by coming to our reception."

The poor people did come to the party out of respect for the king. But some of them showed their disrespect by coming without wedding clothes. The king had them thrown out of the reception.

Jesus told those listening, "Just like the wedding party, there will be many who have been invited to Heaven, but because they show disrespect to my heavenly Father, they will not be allowed to enter. Only those who respect God and his laws will enter Heaven."

? discussion questions

1. What excuses did the people make for not coming to the party?
2. We can show our respect for God by attending church. How else can we show our respect to God?

Story Pictures

What you need

- card stock
- scissors
- resealable plastic sandwich bags, one for each child
- crayons or markers
- adhesive-backed magnets
- magnet board or cookie sheet

What you do

1. For each child, photocopy this page and cut out each set of story pictures. Older children may be able to cut for themselves. Place each set in a separate plastic bag.

2. Follow instructions to prepare a set of story-picture magnets ahead of time.

3. Children color the pictures.

4. Children stick a magnet on the backs of the pictures.

5. As children work, briefly tell the story, placing the story-picture magnets you prepared on the magnet board or a cookie sheet.

6. If time allows, volunteers take a turn telling the story with their own pictures. Or form teams so the team members can tell the stories to each other.

7. Children place magnets in plastic bag to take home.

Tip: As children tell the story, use your story-picture magnets to guide them.

What's the Gift?

What you need

- scissors
- crayons or markers
- glue
- gift bows, one for each child.

What you do

1. For each child, photocopy this page and cut out gift pattern and heart. Older children may be able to cut for themselves.
2. Children color their gifts and hearts.
3. Children fold the gifts on the dashed lines.
4. Children glue the heart inside the gift.
5. Give each child a bow to put on their gift.
6. Demonstrate how to lift the "lid" to see the gift we can give others.

What to Say

The gift boxes we made contain the gift of respect. We can give respect to others. The word *respect* is shown inside the heart. What do hearts remind us of? (Love.) Showing others respect is a way to show God's love!

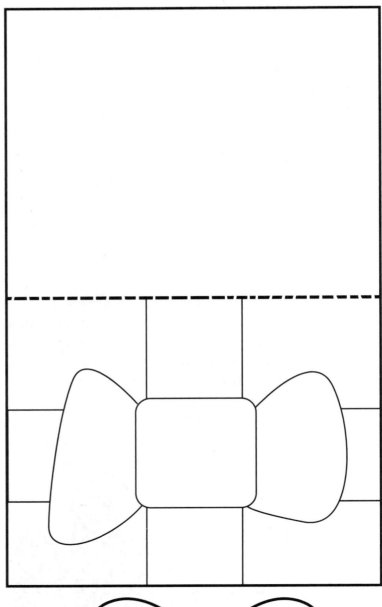

Party Hat

What you need

- construction paper or card stock
- scissors
- glue
- stickers
- crayons or markers
- stapler
- clear tape

What to do

1. For each child, photocopy this page onto construction paper or card stock. Cut out triangle and hearts. Older children may be able to cut for themselves.

2. From construction paper or card stock, cut an 11x2-inch strip for each child.

3. Follow directions to make a sample hat.

4. Children glue the hearts in order on the triangles. Show the hat you prepared as a reference.

5. Children decorate their hats using stickers and crayons or markers.

6. Staple one end of a strip to a triangle. Measure the strip to the child's head and staple the other end of the strip to the triangle. Cut off excess and cover the staples with tape.

Optional: Cut out hearts using decorative-edged scissors.

What to Say

Our party hats remind us of the party in today's story. They also remind us that we can show respect to others.

Parable of the Great Banquet

Come to the Party (based on Matthew 22:1–14)

memory verse

Respect everyone. 1 Peter 2:17

discussion questions

1. What excuses did the people make for not coming to the party?

2. We can show our respect for God by attending church. How else can we show our respect to God?

Give Respect

Children draw pictures of themselves in the square. Discuss each authority figure shown and ask children to name ways to show respect to each one. Children draw lines from their pictures to the authority figures to whom they will show respect.

pastor

fire fighter

parents or guardians

police

teacher

coach

doctor

Parable of the Good Samaritan

memory verse

Love your neighbor. Matthew 5:43

A Good Neighbor (based on Luke 10:25–37)

One day, a lawyer asked Jesus, "You say we should respect and love our neighbors, but who is our neighbor and how do we respect and love them?" Jesus answered his question with a story:

Clip clop, clip clop. Down the road went James. He had come from Jerusalem and was traveling to Jericho. *Clip clop*, went his donkey.

Suddenly from behind the rocks came shouts. James turned around quickly. Robbers! He tried to hurry on, but there were too many of them, and they were too fast.

The robbers beat the man and took his clothes, his donkey, and all he had. "Ohhh," groaned the man, aching all over. "Ohhh, someone help me."

A priest going by heard the man's groans and saw his wounds. *I'm too important to help him*, the priest said to himself. He crossed over to the other side of the road and left.

Next, a Levite heard the man's groans. He looked to see where the groans were coming from. *I can't help him*, he thought. *I'm a busy man.* He, too, crossed to the other side of the road and left.

Later, coming down the road, a Samaritan saw something lying by the road. Quickly getting off his donkey, he went to the man. *This man needs help*, he said to himself.

Gently, the Samaritan cleaned the blood and dirt from the man's wounds and rubbed oil into the sores. He tore some linen cloth into bandages and wrapped them around the wounds. Then the Samaritan put the wounded man on his donkey and took him to the nearest inn. "Look after this man," he told the innkeeper, giving him some money. "If this isn't enough, I will return and give you more."

"Everyone is our neighbor," Jesus told the lawyer. "Remember this story, and respect others the way the Samaritan did."

discussion questions

1. Why should we love the neighbor who lives next door?

2. Who is your neighbor?

A Kind Neighbor

What you need

- scissors or papercutter
- crayons or markers
- small adhesive bandages
- glue

What to do:

1. For each child, photocopy this page and cut out the wounded man and the donkey. Older children may be able to cut for themselves.
2. Children color the wounded man and the donkey.
3. Children stick small adhesive bandages on the wounded man.
4. Children glue the man on the donkey.

What to Say

There are many ways you can help your neighbor. Giving your neighbor a hug when they are feeling bad is like giving them a bandage for their wounds.

Top 50 Creative Bible Lessons: Fun Activities for Preschoolers

Happy Bandages

What you need

- scissors or papercutter
- crayons or markers
- glue
- wiggle eyes
- adhesive bandages

What you do

Photocopy and cut out the picture packet for each child.

1. Children color the packet and complete the drawing of a face, except for the eyes.
2. Children fold the paper on the dashed line to form a packet.
3. Children glue on wiggle yes and then glue together the sides and bottom edges of the packet. Children leave the top edges open.
4. Give each child a few adhesive bandages to place inside the packet

What to Say

Whenever you use the bandages you put in your packet, remember the good Samaritan and "Love your neighbor" (Matthew 5:43).

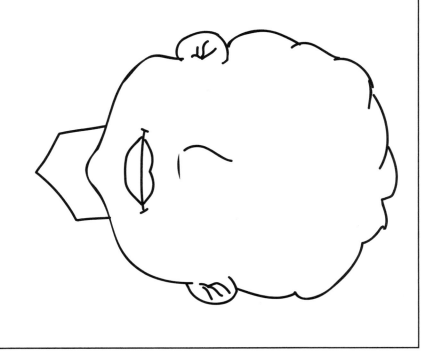

Happy Neighbor

What you need

- scissors
- crayons or markers
- tall glasses
- cranberry-raspberry juice
- raspberry sherbet
- ice-cream scoop
- lemon soda water
- drinking straws

What you do

1. Photocopy and cut out one coaster for each child.

2. Children color their coasters.

3. For each child, half-fill a cup with cranberry-raspberry juice. Add a small scoop of raspberry sherbet. Pour lemon soda over the top.

4. Serve with a straw and watch for the bubbles!

What to Say

Do you know that helping others makes you happy? When you help pick up sticks or leaves in your neighbor's yard, your heart feels bubbly. When you help feed the neighbor's dog, your heart feels bubbly. It bubbles because it is happy.

Parable of the Good Samaritan

A Good Neighbor (based on Luke 10:25–37)

memory verse

Love your neighbor. Matthew 5:43

discussion questions

1. Why should we love the neighbor who lives next door?

2. Who is your neighbor?

Verse Words

Children draw a picture above the verse to show how they can show respect to their neighbor.
(Some ideas: rake leaves, play nice together, share flowers, sweep the porch, share cookies.)

Matthew 5:43

Loaves and Fishes

memory verse

Don't forget to do good and to share with those in need. Hebrews 13:16

Food for a Crowd (based on Mark 6:30–44)

Jesus was tired. He had been preaching to crowds and healing the sick for many, many days.

"Let's get away and rest," Jesus told his friends. So they got on their boat and sailed across the Sea of Galilee.

But Jesus didn't get much time to rest. The crowds of people followed him because they knew he could heal them.

Jesus saw that the people needed healing and needed to be taught about God. Jesus spent much of the day talking to the crowd and healing those who needed it.

A small boy in the crowd saw Jesus doing these miracles. He saw a man who had a bad leg now walking around. He saw a blind woman looking with joy at her young son. He saw Jesus touch the ears of a man who couldn't hear— and then the man suddenly began to hear and talk!

This small boy knew Jesus was God's Son. When Jesus' friends began looking for food for the people, he looked at his small lunch of five barley rolls and two small fish. It wasn't much, but he wanted to give it to Jesus.

Jesus took the boy's small lunch and thanked God for it. Then he told his helpers to pass the food around to all the people. The boy watched as the food turned into enough for everyone to eat, and there were twelve baskets left over. All from his tiny lunch!

 discussion questions

1. Why did the little boy know Jesus could use his small lunch?

2. What are some of the other miracles Jesus performed?

Count the Fish

What you need

- scissors or papercutter
- crayons or markers

What you do

1. For each child, photocopy this page and cut out activity. Older children may be able to cut for themselves.
2. Children look at the numbers on the baskets and find the people holding the corresponding numbers of fish.
3. Children color each basket and the matching person the same color.

What to Say

How many fish did the boy bring to Jesus? Why do you think he was willing to share his lunch?

Sharing with Others

What you need

- scissors or papercutter
- crayons or markers

What to do

1. For each child, photocopy this page and cut out the activity. Older children may be able to cut for themselves.

2. Children count the shapes and write the total in the boxes.

3. Children color the picture.

What to Say

In the Bible story, the boy shared his lunch. Jesus shows us other examples of sharing. Jesus shared his time. He shared his knowledge. He shared his love! How can you share with someone today?

 Top 50 Creative Bible Lessons: Fun Activities for Preschoolers

Not in Bible Times

What you need

- scissors or papercutter
- crayons or markers

What to do:

1. For each child, photocopy this page and cut out the activity. Older children may be able to cut for themselves.
2. Discuss the pictures. Ask children to find and circle five things that would not have been found in Bible days.
3. Children color the pictures.

What to Say

Even though we don't live the same way as people in Bible times, we still praise Jesus just like they did.

Jesus still does miracles for us! Jesus will make us better when we are sick, and he will provide food for us when we are hungry, just like he did in Bible times.

Answers:
1. skates
2. skateboard
3. airplane
4. headphones/ cell phone
5. suit and tie

Loaves and Fishes

Food for a Crowd (based on Mark 6:30–44)

memory verse

Don't forget to do good and to share with those in need. Hebrews 13:16

discussion questions

1. Why did the little boy know Jesus could use his small lunch?

2. What are some of the other miracles Jesus performed?

Game Cube

Cut the pattern from the page. Fold along the lines to form a box. Glue the tabs or tape the seams.

To play, players take turns tossing the game cube.

If the cube shows a fish, all players must make fish faces. Take pictures!

If the cube shows a picture of Jesus, player who tossed the cube names something you can pray about.

If the cube shows a picture of a loaf of bread, player who tossed the cube says one of their favorite foods.

Consider changing what players do when the cube lands on a fish, Jesus, or loaf of bread. The options can include answering a question or doing something physical, individual or group response, serious or silly—it's all your pick!

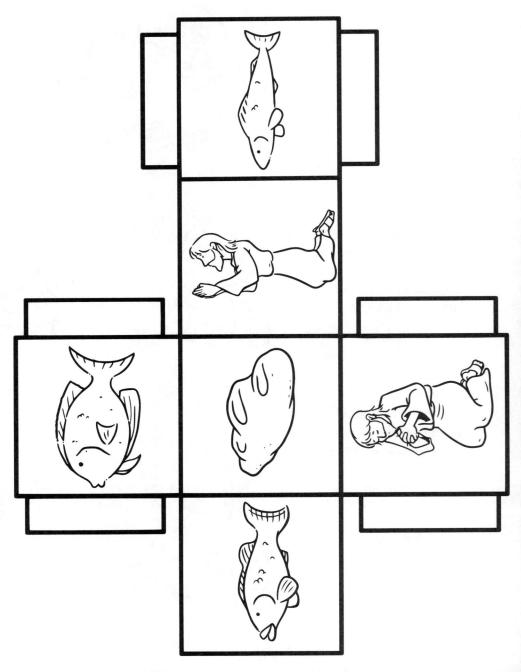

 Top 50 Creative Bible Lessons: Fun Activities for Preschoolers

Jairus's Daughter

memory verse

O LORD, you are our Father. Isaiah 64:8

CHAPTER 33

A Father's Love (based on Luke 8:40–56)

As Jesus traveled from town to town, many people crowded around him, wanting to be healed. One day, a man named Jairus came to Jesus and begged him to come to his house. He said his only daughter, who was twelve years old, was dying. Jairus knew Jesus could heal his daughter.

But as Jesus was traveling to Jairus' house, someone told them that Jairus' daughter had died already. It was too late for Jesus . . . or so they thought!

Jesus told Jairus, "Don't be afraid; only believe, and she will be healed." Jairus believed. They continued traveling to Jarius' house.

Jairus' little girl was in bed when Jesus arrived. Her family was crying because they were very sad that she died. Jesus told everyone, "Stop crying. She is not dead, but asleep." Many laughed at him.

Jesus took her by the hand and said, "My child, get up!" The little girl stood up. She wasn't dead. Jesus had made her well!

The girl's parents were very happy. They were amazed at the miracle, and they believed in Jesus.

Jairus was a loving father to his daughter. Jesus helped Jairus because God had sent him to Earth to help us. God sent Jesus to Earth because God is a loving Father to all of us.

 discussion questions

1. How did Jairus show love to his daughter?
2. How does it make you feel to know that God is your Father?

A Girl's Bed

What you need

- scissors or papercutter
- crayons or markers
- 3×3-inch sticky notes

What to do

1. For each child, photocopy this page and cut out girl figure and bed. Older children may be able to cut for themselves.

2. Children color girl figure and her bed, and then fold bed on dotted line.

3. Give each child a sticky note to place on top of the bed as a cover.

4. Children place girl in bed, cover her by folding cover, and uncover her again.

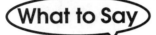

Breifly retell story as children use their figures and beds to act out the story action. **When you don't feel well, you can ask God to help you feel better. God is our Father who loves and cares for us.**

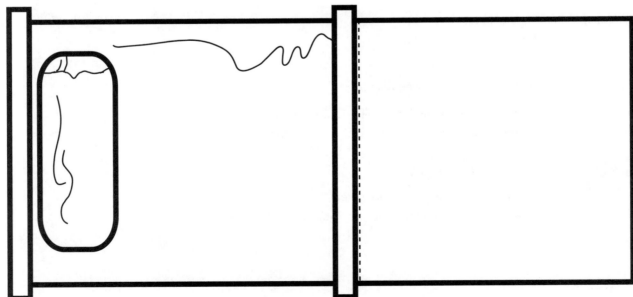

Circle the Differences

What you need

- scissors or papercutter
- crayons or markers

What to do

1. For each child, photocopy this page and cut out activity. Older children may be able to cut for themselves.

2. Children circle the four differences between the two images of Jairus's daughter.

What to Say

After Jesus healed the little girl, Jairus and his family were so amazed! They had been sad, but Jesus gave them a special gift — their little girl was well!

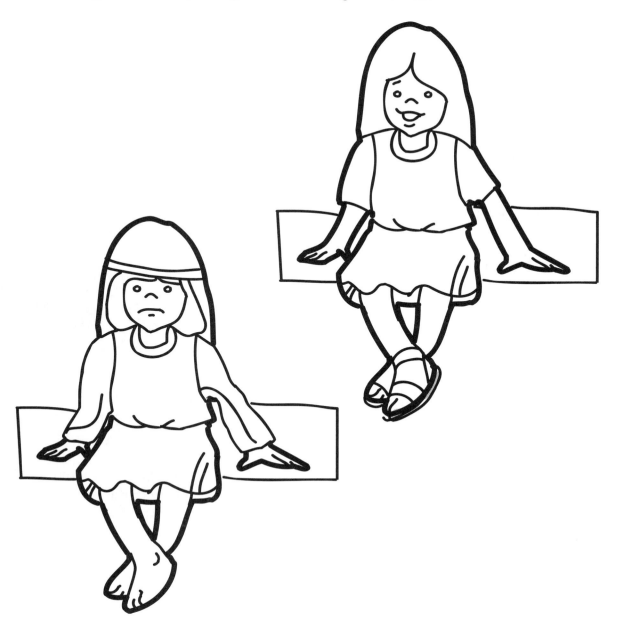

Jesus Helped a Little Girl

What you need

- scissors or papercutter
- crayons or markers

What to do

1. Photocopy this page to use as reference as you teach the song and finger play to children.

2. Sing "Jesus Helped a Girl" song with children to the tune of "Mary Had a Little Lamb."

3. Say the "Come Quickly" verse with children a few times. Use these motions for key phrases.

Whenever you say: "Come quickly," make a beckoning motion.

"Believe," point to your temple.

"Get up," raise hands over head.

"She's well," jump up and down.

Jesus Helped a Girl

A little girl was sick one day
Sick one day
Sick one day
A little girl was sick one day
Go ask Jesus to help her.

Jesus was walking along the way
Along the way
Along the way
Jesus was walking along the way
Jesus please come help her.

Jesus went to help the girl
Help the girl
Help the girl
Jesus went to help the girl
Because Jairus believed.

Jesus told the girl to rise
Girl to rise
Girl to rise
Jesus told the girl to rise
Then she was all well.

Come Quickly

Come quickly! Come quickly!
A daddy said to Jesus.

Come quickly! Come quickly!
My little girl is sick.

Believe! Believe!
Jesus said, "Just believe."

Get up! Get up!
Jesus said, "Get up."

She's well! She's well!
A happy daddy said,
"She's well!"

Jairus's Daughter

A Father's Love (based on Luke 8:40–56)

 memory verse

O LORD, you are our Father. Isaiah 64:8

 discussion questions

1. How did Jairus show love to his daughter?

2. How does it make you feel to know that God is your Father?

Jesus Helps Jairus's Daughter

Color the picture of Jesus healing Jairus's daughter.

Top 50 Creative Bible Lessons: Fun Activities for Preschoolers.

Jesus Blesses the Children

memory verse

See how very much our Father loves us, for he calls us his children. 1 John 3:1

Bring Them to Me (based on Mark 10:13–16)

Jesus was very different from the other religious leaders. They cared more about how they looked and acted than about the love in their hearts. Those who heard Jesus preach and watched him work miracles loved him immediately. Even when he spoke about something that was difficult for the people to hear, Jesus' eyes were filled with love.

The people knew that Jesus thought children were important, too. So these parents decided to take their children to Jesus and ask him to pray for them. But when Jesus' friends saw all the women with their small children, Jesus' friends waved them away.

"Jesus is busy," one of them said. "Don't waste his time."

Jesus heard the disciple. In anger, Jesus said, "Don't ever send children away from me."

Then Jesus motioned for the children to come nearer.

"See these children?" Jesus asked. "The kingdom of Heaven belongs to those who are as willing to believe as these boys and girls do. They are humble, and you will need their kind of humility to enter Heaven."

Then Jesus stretched out his arms and hugged the children to him. The parents smiled. They knew this was one day the boys and girls would never forget. They would always feel Jesus' arms of love around them.

 ## discussion questions

1. Why did Jesus say to let the children come to him?
2. How does it feel to know that Jesus loves you?

Find the Shadow

What you need

- scissors or papercutter
- crayons or markers

What to do:

1. Photocopy this page and cut out activity. Older children may be able to cut for themselves.

2. Children draw a line from each picture to its shadow.

What to Say

Each one of us is different, so our shadows are different. But there's one thing we all have the same: Jesus loves us, each and every one!

Turn to the child next to you and find something that is different about that person. (Joshua) says (Alexander) is different because he (has brown hair and Joshua's hair is blond). Now, let's say together, "Jesus loves us all!"

Bring Them to Me

What you need

- scissors or papercutter
- crayons or markers

What to do

1. For each child, photocopy this page and cut out rectangle.
Older children may be able to cut for themselves.

2. Color the pictures of Jesus and the children.

3. Bring the children to Jesus by folding on the dashed lines.

4. As children color, sing "Jesus Loves Me" or another related song.

Jesus loves
children.

Jesus loves
me.

Blessings Puzzle

What you need

- white card stock
- scissors or papercutter
- crayons or markers

What to do

1. On card stock, photocopy this page and cut out puzzle picture, but do not cut on the dashed lines. Older children may be able to cut for themselves.

2. Children color the picture of Jesus and the children.

3. Cut the picture apart on the dashed lines.

4. Put your picture puzzle back together to remember that Jesus loves children and Jesus loves you!

Jesus Blesses the Children

Bring Them to Me (based on Mark 10:13–16)

memory verse

See how very much our Father loves us, for he calls us his children. 1 John 3:1

discussion questions

1. Why did Jesus say to let the children come to him?

2. How does it feel to know that Jesus loves you?

Jesus and Me

Connect the dashed lines to see who loves you. Draw a picture of your family next to Jesus. Then color the picture. Remember that Jesus loves everyone in your family.

One Man Said Thanks

memory verse

Give thanks to the LORD, for he is good! His faithful love endures forever. 1 Chronicles 16:34

Thank You, Jesus (based on Luke 17:12–19)

"Jesus is coming through here!" At the words of the man, nine other men were suddenly as still as mice. Finally one spoke, "Jesus is coming, you say?"

These ten men had leprosy, a terrible sickness, and they had heard wonderful things about Jesus and his power to heal. Could it be possible they would be healed? The lepers were filled with hope as they quickly walked as close to the road as they were allowed.

Lepers were not allowed to be near the road where people would be walking so they wouldn't spread the dreaded disease. When the lepers saw Jesus, they had to call loudly, "Jesus, Jesus, please have mercy on us. Take away our leprosy, Jesus."

Jesus turned and looked at the men. Their capes had hoods that covered their heads. They had scarves around their faces. This was so no one would have to look at their horrible sores.

"Yes," answered Jesus. "I will heal you. Go and show the priests that you are healed of your disease."

The ten men ran quickly toward town. They knew that as soon as the priest saw that they were healed from their dreadful disease, they could go back home.

All of a sudden, one man stopped. Jesus had healed him, and he had forgotten to even say thank you. Running back to where Jesus was, he kneeled down. "Jesus, thank you. Thank you for healing me," he said.

Jesus looked around. "It is good that you are thankful, but where are the others? Didn't I heal ten men?"

Only one healed leper was thankful.

discussion questions

1. Do you sometimes forget to thank God for what he does for you?

2. What will you thank God for today?

Going Back

What you need

- scissors or papercutter
- crayons or markers

What you do

1. For each child, photocopy this page and cut out the maze. Older children may be able to cut for themselves.

2. Children follow the path from the thankful man to Jesus with a crayon or marker.

3. Children color the picture.

What to Say

Breifly retell story as children find their way through the maze and color the pictures. **Only one man thanked Jesus for making him well. We can thank Jesus every day for his love and care.**

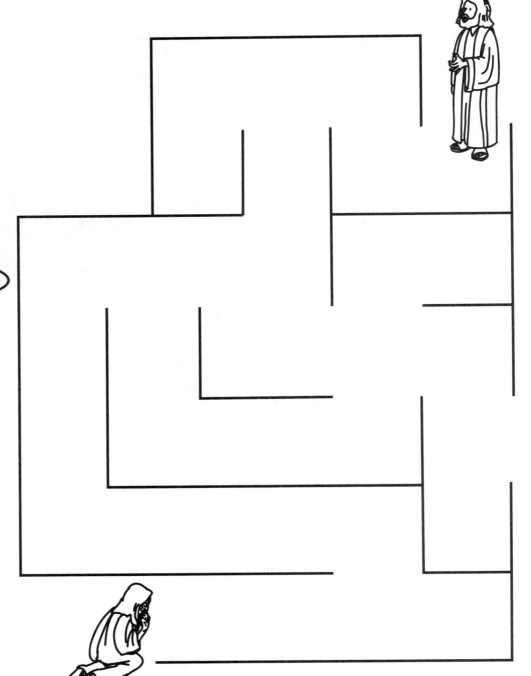

I'm Thankful For...

What you need

- scissors or papercutter
- snack items

What you do

1. Photocopy and cut out the thankful item squares from this page.

2. Lay all of them, except the food, face down on the table.

3. One-by-one have a child pick up a paper and say, "I am thankful for . . ." and then complete the sentence with the name of the object on their paper.

4. When the last item is chosen, hold up the food and say, **I am thankful for food, are you? I have a snack for all of you, so let's thank God for all these things, and let's thank him for our snack, too.**

What to Say

Jesus, we want to thank You for all of the blessings You give us. We thank You for . . . Children taking turns saying the name of the item they picked. **In Jesus' name, amen.**

Thankful Man Runs Back

What you need

- scissors
- crayons or markers

What to do

1. Photocopy this page and cut out thankful man finger puppet. Cut out the leg openings. Older children may be able to cut out the puppet for themselves, but they may need help with the leg openings.
2. Children color the finger puppets
3. Demonstrate how to put your fingers through the holes of the puppet and make the leper run.
4. Sing the song to the tune of "Row, Row, Row Your Boat." While singing, children pretend to make the leper run toward town, and then run him back to say "Thank you" and kneel in front of Jesus.

Run, run, run to town.
Tell the happy news.
Oops, I forgot to thank my Lord.
I stop and turn around.

Run, run, run to say,
Thank you, precious Lord.
Thank you for your healing touch.
I praise your name today!

One Man Said Thanks

Thank You, Jesus (based on Luke 17:12–19)

memory verse

Give thanks to the LORD, for he is good! His faithful love endures forever. 1 Chronicles 16:34

discussion questions

1. Do you sometimes forget to thank God for what he does for you?

2. What will you thank God for today?

Thank You

Read the story with children. Then, children color the boxes of things for which they are thankful.

parents

friends

home

One, two, three, four, five, six, seven, eight, nine, ten men had leprosy. They couldn't come near anyone while they were sick.

One, two, three, four, five, six, seven, eight, nine, ten men saw Jesus and yelled, "Make us well!"

Jesus said, "Go show yourselves to the priests."

When one, two, three, four, five, six, seven, eight, nine, ten men went away, they were made well.

Even though one, two, three, four, five, six, seven, eight, nine, ten men were made well, one man turned and came back.

"Thank you, Jesus," he said.

"Where are the other one, two, three, four, five, six, seven, eight, nine?" Jesus asked.

Only one man came back to thank Jesus.

food

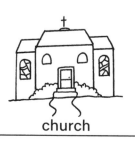
church

Jesus

The Rich Young Ruler

memory verse

Don't love money. Hebrews 13:5

More Than Money (based on Luke 18:18–23)

There was a young ruler who had everything a man could want. He was also being trained to become a religious leader. But this young man felt sad in his heart. There was something missing from his life.

I know, thought the young ruler. *I'll go ask Jesus. He knows the answer to every question.*

When the young ruler found out where Jesus was, he ran up to him. Kneeling and bowing his head, the man asked, "Lord, what must I do to get to Heaven? I want to live forever."

Jesus said, "You need to follow the commandments of God."

The young ruler nodded. "I have, Jesus. I have kept the commandments since I was a small boy."

Jesus took the man's hand and pulled him to his feet. "Then there is just one thing more you must do," Jesus said.

"Tell me, Jesus," he said. "I'll do whatever you say."

Jesus knew the young ruler meant what he was saying, but Jesus also knew that he loved having money and the things his money bought. Jesus knew that as important as God was to the young ruler, his possessions were even more important.

Jesus said, "If you want to live forever with me in Heaven, you must sell all that you have and give your money to the poor."

"But they're mine," he said. "The things I have are mine!"

"Are they more important than me?" asked Jesus.

Without a word, the young ruler turned and walked away. He wouldn't give his things up for Jesus.

discussion questions

1. What was the first thing Jesus told the young ruler he must do to get to Heaven?
2. What was the young ruler unwilling to give up for Jesus?

Hidden Toys

What you need
- scissors or papercutter
- crayons or markers

What to do:
1. For each child, photocopy this page and cut out activity. Older children may be able to cut for themselves.

2. Children search for and circle the eight hidden objects in the picture.

3. Children draw a heart around Jesus.

4. Children color the picture.

What to Say

Some things that may be important to you are hidden in the picture. Find a car, truck, toothbrush, doll, purse, teddy bear, teapot, and dog. Circle each object you find.

Next, find who should be the most important of all. Who is he? Draw a heart around Jesus.

Top 50 Creative Bible Lessons: Fun Activities for Preschoolers.

Sad Young Man

What you need

- scissors or papercutter
- glue
- pennies
- crayons or markers

What to do:

1. For each child, photocopy this page and cut out the solid-man piece and the puzzle pieces. Older children may be able to cut for themselves.

2. Give each child a copy of the man shape and a set of puzzle pieces. Children glue the pieces in the correct place on the solid man.

3. Say, **What was more important to this man than loving and obeying Jesus?** (His money and the things his money could buy.) **Glue a penny in the man's hand to remind you not to be like this sad young man.**

4. Children color the finished puzzle.

 Top 50 Creative Bible Lessons: Fun Activities for Preschoolers

Give Your All

What you need

- scissors or papercutter
- crayons or markers
- hole punch
- brads (paper fasteners), one for each child
- transparent tape

What you do

1. For each child, photocopy and cut out a set of pictures.
2. Children color the pictures.
3. Assist children to punch holes where indicated and thread brads through the holes to fasten the book pages together.
4. Cover the ends of the fasteners with tape to prevent injury.

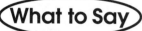

What to Say

There are many ways that giving to God helps us. Giving our money is one way. It reminds us to love God more than money or the things money can buy.

The Rich Young Ruler

More Than Money (based on Luke 18:18–23)

 memory verse

Don't love money. Hebrews 13:5

 discussion questions

1. What was the first thing Jesus told the young ruler he must do to get to Heaven?

2. What was the young ruler unwilling to give up for Jesus?

They're Mine!

Jesus wants us to enjoy the things we have. But in our story, Jesus knew the rich young ruler's things were too important to him. That's why Jesus asked him to give away those things. Jesus knows the very best life begins with loving God more than anything.

In each row, circle the two objects that are exactly the same. Color all the pictures.

The Samaritan Woman

memory verse

Now you are my friends. John 15:15

Living Water (based on John 4:1–39)

Jesus was taking a trip. He was going from Samaria to Judea. Jesus' friends were with him. "I'm getting hungry," one of them said.

"Let's rest here," said Jesus, pointing to a well. "We can get some food and drink."

Jesus' disciples went into the town to get some food. Jesus sat down on the edge of the well to rest and wait. A Samaritan woman came to the well to get some water.

"Hi!" said Jesus. "I'm thirsty. Could you give me a drink of water?"

The woman was surprised that Jesus talked to her. "Why are you talking to me? You are a Jew, and Jews don't talk to Samaritans."

Jesus knew everyone was important to God, no matter who they were, what they looked like, or what they owned.

Jesus offered the woman at the well *living water* so that she would never be thirsty again. She didn't understand at first, but Jesus was talking about himself. Jesus was telling her that being his friend would help her so much more than a drink of water!

Jesus also told her about the bad things she had done in her life. She was amazed that he knew so much about her! He knew her better than her own friends did. She finally realized that Jesus was the Savior God had promised to send.

She left her jar at the well and ran into the town to tell others that she had just met Jesus, the Savior.

 ## discussion questions

1. How did Jesus show he was a friend to the Samaritan woman?
2. When are times you can be friendly to others?

Friend Song

What you need
- none

What to do

1. Photocopy this page to use as reference as you teach the song to children.

2. Sing the song below to help children remember the Bible story of the Samaritan Woman and that Jesus is their friend.

3. Children sing the song and do motions with you as time and interest allow.

Jesus Is My Friend
Sing to the tune of "Good Night, Ladies."

He is my friend.   *point to self*

point to self   He is my friend.

He is my friend.   *point to self*

point to others   Jesus is your friend, too.

Friendship Bracelets

What you need

- scissors or papercutter
- crayons or markers
- transparent tape

What to do

1. For each child, photocopy this page and cut out two bracelets. Older children may be able to cut for themselves
2. Children color their bracelets.
3. Help children place one bracelet around their wrist and tape it closed.
4. Help children tape the other bracelet into a circle.

What to Say

One bracelet reads, "Jesus is my friend!!" That bracelet is for you to wear as a reminder.

The other bracelet says, "Jesus is your friend!!" That bracelet is for a friend. Who is someone who needs to know that Jesus is their friend? You can give this bracelet to that person!

CUT

JESUS IS MY FRIEND!!

JESUS IS YOUR FRIEND!!

Hello at the Well

What you need

- scissors
- crayons or markers
- glue
- hole punch
- brads (paper fasteners), one for each child

What to do

1. For each child, photocopy this page and cut out Jesus figure, arms, and the well. Older children may be able to cut for themselves.
2. Children color the different pattern pieces.
3. Children glue Jesus to be sitting on the well.
4. Help children as needed to punch holes in the Jesus figure and arms as indicated.
5. Children push a brad through the holes and open the spikes.

What to Say

The Bible tells us Jesus is our friend. You can move the arms of the craft you made today. If you move them, it looks like Jesus is waving his arms. Waving to others is a way to be friendly. Let's wave our arms to each other to show that we are being friendly.

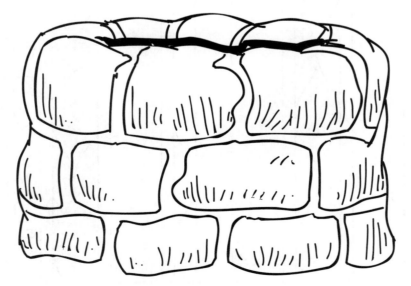

The Samaritan Woman

Living Water (based on John 4:1–39)

memory verse

Now you are my friends. John 15:15

discussion questions

1. How did Jesus show he was a friend to the Samaritan woman?

2. When are times you can be friendly to others?

A Friend to All

Color the picture of Jesus being friendly to the woman at the well.

Zacchaeus Climbs a Tree

memory verse

O Lord, you are so good, so ready to forgive. Psalm 86:5

Zacchaeus Sees Jesus (based on Luke 19:1–10)

Everyone wanted to see Jesus. Word had spread that Jesus was coming through Jericho. Excitement filled the air as men and women tried to push through the crowd so they could be sure to see Jesus.

One little, short man named Zacchaeus tried to push his way through the crowd. *I'll never be able to see over everyone,* he thought to himself. "If only I were taller," he said out loud as people deliberately blocked his way. But it wasn't only his size that kept people from letting him through. Nobody liked Zacchaeus.

Zacchaeus was a tax collector. He was very rich because he collected money for the Romans. Zacchaeus would make the taxpayers pay extra to him. Zacchaeus was growing rich because he was cheating others.

Zacchaeus was frustrated when everywhere he turned seemed blocked, so he decided to see Jesus another way. He climbed up in one of the big sycamore trees that were planted along the road to provide shade for tired travelers. "Now I can see," he said. Sure enough, there was Jesus walking down the dusty road. Closer and closer Jesus walked. *He looks so kind,* Zacchaeus thought. *I wonder if he would love a sinner like me?*

Just then Jesus stopped under the tree where Zacchaeus was sitting. Zacchaeus was so surprised he nearly fell out of the tree! "Zacchaeus," said Jesus in a soft, kind voice. "Come down from the tree. I want to go to your house."

Jesus wasn't at his house very long before Zacchaeus knew that Jesus loved him. He wanted to be like Jesus. Zacchaeus said, "I will not only give back the money I have taken from people, but I will give them back four times the amount."

Jesus was happy, too. Jesus knew Zacchaeus had changed. Instead of wanting to take away from people, Zacchaeus wanted to give! Jesus forgave Zacchaeus for the wrong things he'd done.

discussion questions

1. How did Jesus show that he cared for Zacchaeus?

2. What did Zacchaeus say that showed he was sorry for the wrong things he'd done?

Count on It

What you need

- scissors or papercutter
- crayons or markers

What to do

1. For each child, photocopy this page and cut out activity. Older children may be able to cut for themselves.

2. Children count the items in each row and write the number next to that row.

3. Children color the pictures.

What to Say

Zacchaeus didn't have many friends because he cheated people. One day, Jesus went to Zacchaeus' town. Zacchaeus decided to become a good person. Zacchaeus paid back four times the amount of money he took! Jesus forgave Zacchaeus for the wrong things he'd done. Zacchaeus was happy to have a friend like Jesus!

     _____

    _____

      _____

Up a Tree

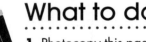

What you need

- scissors or papercutter
- crayons or markers

What to do

1. Photocopy this page and cut out activity. Older children may be able to cut for themselves.

2. Children connect the dots and color the picture.

What to Say

Zacchaeus climbed the tree to see Jesus. He knew that Jesus was kind. Jesus showed he was a friend to Zacchaeus by going to his house and by forgiving him. Jesus wants to forgive you, too!

Coin Match-Up

What you need

- scissors or papercutter
- crayons or markers

What to do

1. For each child, photocopy this page and cut out matching activity.
Older children may be able to cut for themselves.

2. Children match the two pieces of coin that go together by drawing a line between them.

What to Say

Zacchaeus was a tax collector. No one liked him because he collected more money than he should. One day, Jesus came to Zacchaeus' town. Jesus forgave Zacchaeus for the wrong things he'd done. Zacchaeus was like a new man! He paid back all the money he'd taken— and even more!

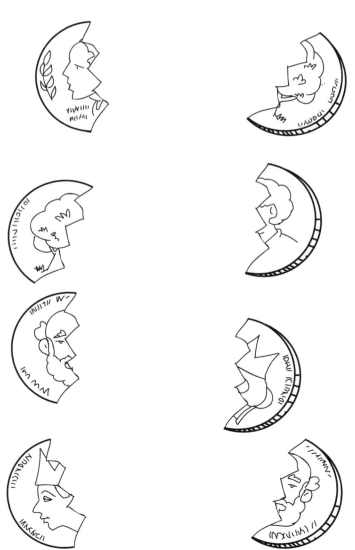

Zacchaeus Climbs a Tree

Zacchaeus Sees Jesus (based on Luke 19:1–10)

memory verse

O Lord, you are so good, so ready to forgive. Psalm 86:5

discussion questions

1. How did Jesus show that he cared for Zacchaeus?

2. What did Zacchaeus say that showed he was sorry for the wrong things he'd done?

Tree Talk

Color the picture of Zacchaeus sitting in the tree, talking with Jesus.

Jesus Enters Jerusalem

memory verse

Sing to the LORD! Praise the LORD! Jeremiah 20:13

Praise the Lord (based on Matthew 20:29—21:17)

Jesus was traveling from Jericho to Jerusalem. Wherever he went, a crowd followed. This particular day, two blind men were along the road Jesus was traveling. As soon as the blind men heard that Jesus was coming, they began shouting.

"Have mercy on us, oh, Lord!" they called as he passed.

Those around them tried to shush them, but Jesus heard.

"What do you want me to do for you?" Jesus asked as he stopped to face them.

"We want to be able to see," the blind men said.

Jesus reached out and touched their eyes. Immediately, they could see Jesus. They looked around to see the crowds. They saw the trees and the blue sky. Then the men joined the crowd following Jesus.

The crowd continued to grow as Jesus rode his donkey into Jerusalem. The people were happy to see Jesus. When Jesus arrived at Jerusalem, he went to the temple to worship. The crowds followed and joined those in the temple who wanted to hear Jesus teach.

They also wanted to see Jesus work miracles. The children began singing about Jesus.

"Hosanna!" they sang in their best praise voices. "Hosanna to the Son of God." Jesus smiled when he heard their songs.

"Listen to the children sing," he told the disciples. "The Bible teaches us that small children sing their praises to God more sweetly than anyone else. Everyone should praise God."

discussion questions

1. How were the children worshiping God in the temple?
2. What are some ways we can worship God with our praise?

King of Kings

![scissors and pencils in cup]

What you need

- scissors or papercutter
- crayons or markers

What to do

1. For each child, photocopy this page and cut out activity. Older children may be able to cut for themselves.

2. Children compare the pictures in each row and circle the picture that looks the same as the first picture in that row.

What to Say

Jesus is our king. He is the King of kings. He is more important than any president or king on Earth. Jesus is God's Son.

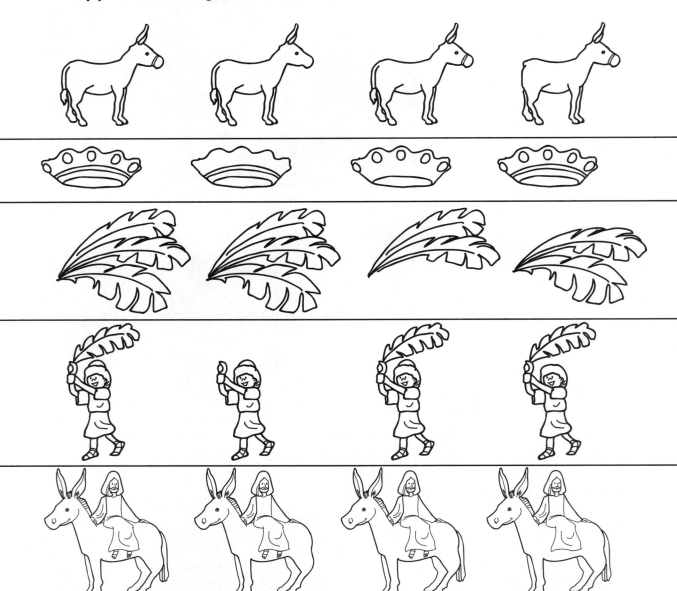

Top 50 Creative Bible Lessons: Fun Activities for Preschoolers

Praise Windsock

What you need

- scissors or papercutter
- yarn
- transparent tape
- crayons or markers
- hole punch

What to do

1. For each child, photocopy this page and cut out windsock patterns. Older children may be able to cut for themselves.
2. Cut three 1×8-inch strips of paper for each child. Cut a 20-inch length of yarn for each child.
3. Make a sample craft to show the children.
4. Each child tapes three paper strips to the back of the page at the bottom.
5. Children color the page.
6. Children fold the page into a triangle shape and tape the edge.
7. Punch two holes along the top edge. Thread yarn through through holes and tie for a hanger.

What to Say

We can praise Jesus like the people in our story did. Hang up your windsock at home as a reminder to praise Jesus.

HOSANNA

SHOUTED

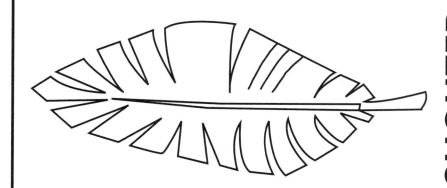

THEY

Jesus Is Coming!

What you need

- scissors or papercutter
- crayons or markers

What to do

1. For each child, photocopy this page and cut out activity.
Older children may be able to cut for themselves.

2. Children color green only the palm leaves,
and then color the rest of the picture.

3. Recite rhyming story with children as they work.

Jesus is coming!

Hosanna! Hosanna!

Jesus is coming to town.

Let's get ready!

Hosanna!

Hosanna!

We have palm branches to wave.

Shout to Jesus!

Hosanna!

Hosanna!

Jesus is the King!

Top 50 Creative Bible Lessons: Fun Activities for Preschoolers

Jesus Enters Jerusalem

Praise the Lord (based on Matthew 20:29—21:17)

memory verse

Sing to the LORD! Praise the LORD! Jeremiah 20:13

discussion questions

1. How were the children worshiping God in the temple?

2. What are some ways we can worship God with our praise?

Jesus Rides a Donkey

Color the donkey and cut it out along the dashed lines. Glue the donkey to a folded sheet of construction paper so the donkey's head and back stick up above the fold and the donkey stands up. Glue a piece of fabric to the donkey's back as a blanket for Jesus to sit on.

The donkey can help you remember to praise Jesus like the people did when Jesus rode into Jerusalem.

place along fold

place along fold

The Last Supper

memory verse

We know what real love is because Jesus gave up his life for us. 1 John 3:16

To Remember (based on Matthew 16:1–46)

The Passover meal was the last meal Jesus ate before he was crucified. He and his friends ate it together in an upstairs room that was prepared for the meal.

While they ate, Jesus told them that one of them would soon betray him, and that one of them would deny knowing him. This was hard for Jesus' friends to understand.

As he spoke, Jesus broke off the bread and shared it with his friends. He also shared a cup of wine with them. Jesus wanted his followers to celebrate this special meal in a new way. He wanted it to remind them of his death. He wanted them to remember that he loved them enough to die for them.

In the evening after the Passover meal, Jesus and his disciples went to the Garden of Gethsemane. Jesus went ahead of the disciples and prayed alone. When he came back to them, he found them sleeping instead of keeping watch and praying.

Jesus was suffering terrible agony because he knew he was going to be killed. But even so, he was willing to suffer in order to save us from our sins.

discussion questions

1. What did Jesus want his friends to remember by eating this special meal?

2. Why was Jesus willing to die for us?

The Bread and the Cup

What you need
- scissors or papercutter
- crayons or markers

What to do
1. For each child, photocopy this page and cut out activity. Older children may be able to cut for themselves.
2. Children color the shapes with letters from the word *remembrance*.

What to Say

Jesus prayed and took some bread and broke it into pieces. He handed the other disciples each a piece. "Eat this," Jesus said. "It will remind you of how my body was broken." Then, he prayed again and took a cup and said, "Drink this cup. It will remind you that I shed my blood for you." Whenever people take communion in church, they are remembering that Jesus loved them so much that he died for their sins.

REMEMBRANCE

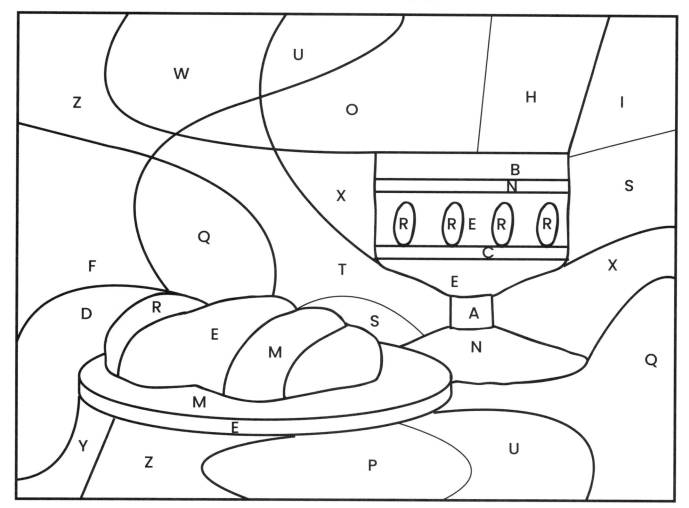

Remember Kabobs

What you need

- scissors or papercutter
- marshmallows
- circle-shaped cereal
- crayons or markers
- stapler
- drinking straw, one for each child

What to do

1. Photocopy this page and cut out verse paper at right.
   Older children may be able to cut for themselves.
2. Place mini-marshmallows and round cereal pieces in bowls
   and place on tables where children will be working.
3. Children color verse paper and then staple to a drinking straw.
   Assist younger children with stapler as needed.
4. Give each child a drinking straw.
5. Children make kabobs by threading a marshmallow on the drinking straw and
   then threading on a piece of cereal. Repeat the pattern until the straw is filled.
6. While the children work, say, **Let's take turns saying
   something we want to remember about Jesus.**
7. Children enjoy their kabobs!

"We know what real love is because Jesus gave up his life for us."

1 John 3:16

Jesus Serves Supper

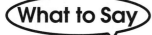

What you need

- scissors
- crayons or markers
- glue
- paper plates, one for each child

What to do

1. For each child, photocopy this page and cut out food items. Older children may be able to cut for themselves.

2. Children color the food items and then glue them to their paper plates.

Enrichment Idea: Children use play dough to make additional food shapes.

What to Say

Jesus told his friends what to do to get ready for a special meal. They obeyed Jesus. Jesus wanted to have this special meal as an example to us to have meals to remember he loved us so much he was willing to die for us.

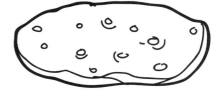

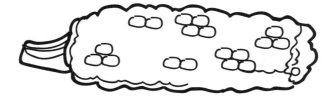

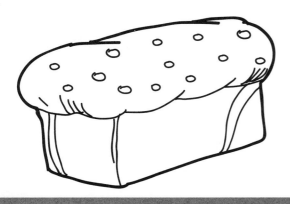

The Last Supper

To Remember (based on Matthew 16:1–46)

memory verse

We know what real love is because Jesus gave up his life for us. 1 John 3:16

discussion questions

1. What did Jesus want his friends to remember by eating this special meal?

2. Why was Jesus willing to die for us?

Jesus' Last Supper

Color the picture of Jesus and his friends eating their last supper together.

Jesus Dies and Lives Again

memory verse

[Jesus] has risen from the dead. Matthew 28:7

It Is Finished (based on Matthew 27:11—28:10)

Even though Jesus traveled around teaching people about God, healing people who were sick or hurt, and showing love to everyone, there were some people who didn't like Jesus. They were angry that God's people liked Jesus so much.

These angry men came up with a mean plan. They lied about Jesus and got him arrested, even though he had done nothing wrong!

Things went so far that Jesus even got killed! Jesus was hung on a cross and left to die. Remember, Jesus is God's Son. He could have stopped all of this. But he willingly chose to give up his life so that we can be forgiven for the wrong things we do. Jesus loves us so much that he died for us!

But Jesus didn't stay dead! Three days later, some of his friends came to visit his tomb. But Jesus wasn't there! Jesus wasn't in the tomb because Jesus is alive!

discussion questions

1. How do you think Jesus' friends felt to know that he was alive again?

2. What are some ways you can show that you're glad that Jesus is alive?

Connect the Dots Cross

What you need

- scissors or papercutter
- crayons or markers

What to do

1. For each child, photocopy this page and cut out dot-to-dot activity.
Older children may be able to cut for themselves.

2. Children connect the dots to see the cross where Jesus died. Then, children color the picture.

What to Say

**Jesus died and came alive again so that we can be forgiven for all the wrong things we do.
When we accept Jesus' forgiveness, we can become members of God's family.**

Top 50 Creative Bible Lessons: Fun Activities for Preschoolers

The Empty Tomb

What you need

- scissors
- ruler
- brown paper
- crayons or markers

- hole punch
- brads (paper fasteners), one for each child

- Easter grass or thin green construction-paper strips

What to do

1. For each child, photocopy this page and cut out activity. Older children may be able to cut for themselves.
2. Cut a 4-inch circle of brown paper to make a paper stone for each child.
3. Children color the pictures.
4. Help children punch holes in the picture (as indicated) and in a paper stone.
5. Children attach the paper stone to the tomb with a brad.
6. Children to glue Easter grass or construction paper strips beside the tomb for grass.

Story Cross

What you need

- scissors or papercutter
- crayons or markers

What to do

1. For each child, photocopy this page and cut out activity. Older children may be able to cut for themselves.

2. Briefly retell the story as children color the cross and the story pictures.

What to Say

Our cross has pictures from today's story. Point to the picture that shows when Jesus was arrested, even though he had done nothing wrong.

We also have a picture of Jesus when he was on the cross. Point to the picture of Jesus on the cross. The lady in the picture is very sad that Jesus is on the cross. Show me a sad face.

Use your fingers to trace the big cross in the middle of the page.

The next picture shows a very surprised guard. Show me a surprised face. Point to what the guard is pointing at. That's right! It's Jesus' tomb, but he's not there. Jesus isn't in the tomb because he is alive!

In the final picture, we see Jesus and some of his friends. They are so happy that Jesus is alive! I'm happy, too! If you're happy like me, show me your biggest smile!

Jesus Dies and Lives Again

It Is Finished (based on Matthew 27:11—28:10)

memory verse

[Jesus] has risen from the dead. Matthew 28:7

discussion questions

1. How do you think Jesus' friends felt to know that he was alive again?

2. What are some ways you can show that you're glad that Jesus is alive?

Born to Die

When God sent Jesus, he came as a baby whose mission was to grow up and die for us on a cross and rise from the dead. It was all part of God's plan to make a way for us to be members of his family. God planned from the beginning to save us from the punishment for sin. Jesus was born to die so that we might live forever in Heaven.

Jesus Appears to His Friends

memory verse

For where two or three gather together as my followers, I am there among them. Matthew 18:20

Have You Caught Any Fish?

(based on John 21:1–14)

Some of Jesus' friends were fishing. They fished all night, but they couldn't catch any fish in their nets.

Early in the morning, someone came along and called out, "Friends, have you caught any fish?"

The men answered no.

The man on the shore said, "Throw your net on the other side of the boat and you will catch some fish."

Jesus' friends threw the net on the other side of the boat. The net became filled with fish! There were so many fish that the net was too heavy to drag inside the boat.

Then the fishermen realized it was

Jesus who called to them from the shore. They hurried to see him.

Peter was so excited, he jumped in the water and swam to the beach! He couldn't wait to see Jesus!

When Jesus' friends got to the beach, they saw that Jesus had started a fire and cooked some fish and bread. Jesus' friends were glad to see him. They were glad to be with their friend Jesus.

 ### discussion questions

1. What happened when the men put their net on the other side of the boat?

2. Who was calling to them from the shore?

Hinged Story

What you need

- scissors or papercutter
- crayons or markers
- tape

What you do

1. Photocopy this page, making one for each child plus an extra for you to use. Cut out each rectangle. Cut the dashed lines on the rectangle with three story pictures. Older children may be able to cut for themselves.

2. Children color the pictures.

3. Then, children tape the large shore scene onto the left edge of the boat picture and fold it back.

4. Children tape the two smaller scenes onto the right edge of the main picture with the net scene on the bottom and Jesus on the top (as in sketch).

5. Briefly retell the story. Start with the main scene showing and the taped parts folded behind the main scene. Flip forward the picture of Jesus when appropriate in the story, and then flip forward the net. Lastly, bring around the scene of Jesus and his friends on the shore.

A Special Breakfast

What you need

- scissors or papercutter
- crayons or markers

What to do

1. For each child, photocopy this page and cut out coloring activity. Older children may be able to cut for themselves.

2. Children draw fish in the net and color the picture.

What to Say

Peter and his friends' net was empty. Then Jesus came along and helped them catch lots of fish. Draw some fish in the empty net.

Jesus' friends were so happy to be with Jesus. Jesus is with us, too, even though we can't see him. Our Bible verse says "Where two or three gather together as my followers, I am there among them." Let's count how many of us are here. And then we'll add one more because Jesus is here, too!

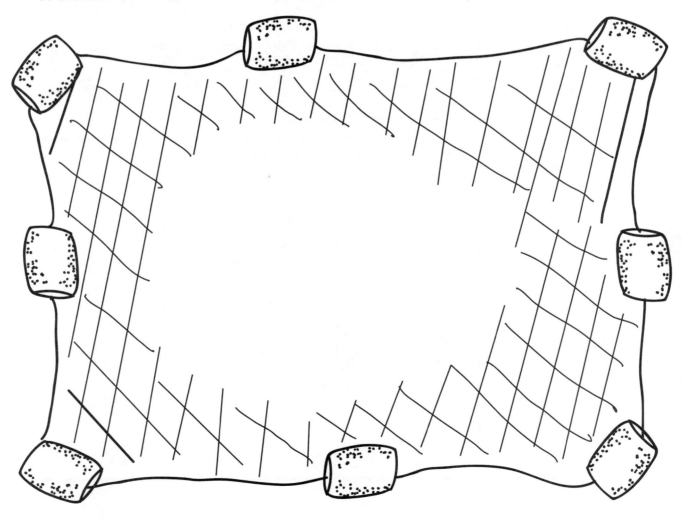

Feed My Sheep

What you need

- scissors or papercutter
- crayons or markers

What to do

1. For each child, photocopy this page and cut out activity. Older children may be able to cut for themselves.
2. Children find the hidden objects described in the key.
3. Children color the picture

What to Say

When Jesus and his friends finished eating breakfast, Jesus asked Peter, "Do you love me?" Peter answered, "Yes, Lord. You know I love you." Jesus said, "Then feed my sheep." Jesus asked again, "Peter, do you love me?" Peter again answered, "Yes, Lord." And Jesus said, "Feed my sheep." Three times Jesus asked Peter the same question and three times Jesus said, "Feed my sheep."

Find 3 🐑, 3 🐟, 3 🍞 and 3 number 3s.

Jesus Appears to His Friends

Have You Caught Any Fish? (based on John 21:1–14)

memory verse

For where two or three gather together as my followers, I am there among them.
Matthew 18:20

discussion questions

1. What happened when the men put their net on the other side of the boat?

2. Who was calling to them from the shore?

Helper Friends

Say the "Jesus Helped" verse with your family, doing motions as shown.

Sing "Friends" with your family to the tune of "Mary Had a Little Lamb."

Jesus Helped

The nets were empty.

hold out empty hands

The fishermen had no fish.

Then Jesus helped his friends.

The nets were full.

pretend hands are full

The fishermen had many fish.

Friends

Jesus helped his friends catch fish,
Friends catch fish,
Friends catch fish.
Jesus helped his friends catch fish.
Jesus is a good friend.

Thank you, God, for giving friends,
Giving friends,
Giving friends.
Thank you, God, for giving friends,
I can help my friends.

Jesus Goes to Heaven

memory verse

We are citizens of heaven. Philippians 3:20

Living with Jesus (based on John 14:1–14, Acts 1:1–11, Revelation)

One day while Jesus was teaching his friends, he told them about Heaven.

He said, "Where my Father lives are many mansions. I am going to prepare one for you."

"But wait a minute," Thomas said to Jesus. "Are you saying we have to find our own way to Heaven?"

"No," Jesus answered. "I am the way to Heaven. If you believe I am the Son of God, then you also know my Father."

Jesus' friends didn't understand what Jesus was saying. But they did know that they believed Jesus was the Son of God.

Soon it was time for Jesus to return to his Father in Heaven. Jesus' friends were sad. Jesus was their best friend. How could they go on without him?

Then something completely amazing happened! Jesus began to rise up into the sky! He disappeared into the clouds.

While Jesus' friends were still looking up to the sky, they heard a voice. "Don't be sad." Two angels were watching them. The angels told Jesus' friends, "Jesus is coming back one day to take you, and all those who believe he is the Son of God, to Heaven with him."

Later, one of Jesus' friends, John, had a dream about Heaven. He saw thousands and thousands of angels singing praise songs to God. He saw beautiful palaces and golden streets.

The vision made John want to be with Jesus in Heaven even more. John knew that Heaven would be a perfect place with no sadness or pain. So he spent the rest of his life telling people how wonderful Heaven would be. He even wrote a book about it. That book is the last one in the Bible. It is called *Revelation*.

discussion questions

1. What do you think Heaven is like?
2. How can you be ready for Heaven?

Finish the Picture

What you need

- scissors or papercutter
- crayons or markers

What you do

1. Photocopy this page for each child and cut out picture. Older children may be able to cut for themselves.
2. Explain to the children that the picture of Heaven seems to be missing a few important things. Name the missing pieces one by one and allow time for the children to fill them in.
3. Children color their pictures.

What to Say

Draw a roof on the mansion with a brown crayon. Draw water in the river with a blue crayon. Draw fruit on the tree with a green crayon. Draw wings on the angel with a yellow crayon. Draw a smile on the child with a red crayon.

 Top 50 Creative Bible Lessons: Fun Activities for Preschoolers

Surprise Snack

What you need

- scissors or papercutter
- crayons or markers
- tall baby food jars
- glue
- milk
- instant pudding
- plastic spoons

What you do

1. Photocopy this page, making one jar wrap for each child.

2. Cut out labels. Older children may be able to cut for themselves.

3. Children color their wraps and glue them around their jars.

4. Pour milk into the jars so they are ¾ full. Add 2 teaspoons of pudding mix to each one.

5. Assist each child in tightly twisting on the cap.

6. Children shake their jars. When the mixtures thicken, give each child a spoon to enjoy the surprise snack.

What to Say

Jesus' friends were surprised when he suddenly rose up into the sky. Let's make a surprise snack to remember that Jesus is in Heaven. One day, as members of God's family, we'll be in Heaven with Jesus!

"We are citizens of heaven."
Philippians 3:20

"We are citizens of heaven."
Philippians 3:20

Count Them All

What you need

- scissors or papercutter
- crayons or markers

What you do

1. Photocopy this page for each child and cut out picture. Older children may be able to cut for themselves.
2. Children color the pictures.
3. Ask, **How many houses do you see in the picture of Heaven, Jesus' home?** Children count the houses.
4. Assist children to print the number in the square with a house.
5. Repeat, counting angels, then clouds, and finally flowers.

What to Say

Members of God's family will live with him in Heaven forever! I'm so glad Jesus made the way for us to become members of God' family.

 Top 50 Creative Bible Lessons: Fun Activities for Preschoolers

Jesus Goes to Heaven

Living with Jesus (based on John 14:1–14, Acts 1:1–11, Revelation)

memory verse

We are citizens of heaven. Philippians 3:20

discussion questions

1. What do you think Heaven is like?

2. How can you be ready for Heaven?

Shoutin' Heaven

Children color the picture below. Then, they add glitter glue to the light rays and stretch out cotton balls to glue on the clouds.

Sing the song "Heaven" to the tune of "The Hokey Pokey."

Heaven

I'll put my happy self in,
I'll put my happy self out,
I'll put my happy self in,
And I'll hop all about.
I'm gonna go to Heaven
And see my Jesus there,
That makes me
want to shout.

HEAVEN!

Philip Teaches about Jesus

memory verse

Preach the Good News to everyone. Mark 16:15

I'll Tell You about Jesus (based on Acts 8:26–39)

After Jesus went to Heaven, his friends went far and wide, telling everyone the good news about Jesus. Philip was one of Jesus' friends. He was preaching in the city of Samaria, telling everyone about Jesus. Many people became followers of Jesus because of what Philip told them.

One day, an angel from God came to Philip. The angel told Philip, "God wants you to leave Samaria and take a road out into the desert." Philip didn't know why God wanted him to leave and go for a walk into the desert, but Philip obeyed God. He left and started walking down the road.

Suddenly, Philip heard something: *clippety-cloppety, clippety-clop.* It was horses! The horses were pulling a chariot. And in the chariot was a man from Ethiopia, a country in Africa. The man was reading a scroll. (A scroll is like a long rolled-up sheet of paper.) Philip realized the man was reading God's Word.

Philip ran up to the chariot. "Do you understand what you are reading?" he asked.

"No." The man responded. "I need someone to explain this to me."

Philip got into the chariot with the man and read God's Word with him. Philip told the man the good news about Jesus. He told how Jesus died and rose again so that we can be forgiven for the wrong things we do. Philip explained how much God loves us and how he wants everyone to be a member of his family.

The man was happy to hear the good news about Jesus. He decided to be forgiven and follow Jesus! The man said, "Look! There's some water. I want to be baptized." Being baptized is a way to let other people know that you are a friend and follower of Jesus.

Philip was glad he was able to tell the man about Jesus and baptize him. Then Philip left the man and went on his way, eager to tell other people about Jesus.

discussion questions

1. What was the man Philip met reading?
2. Who did Philip teach the man about?

Philip Obeys God

What you need

- scissors or papercutter
- crayons or markers

What to do

1. For each child, photocopy this page and cut out maze. Older children may be able to cut for themselves.

2. Children find their way through the maze to get Philip to the man from Ethiopia

What to Say

God sent an angel to Philip. The angel told Philip to go south. On his journey, Philip met an Ethiopian. Philip taught this man about Jesus. The man decided to follow Jesus, too.

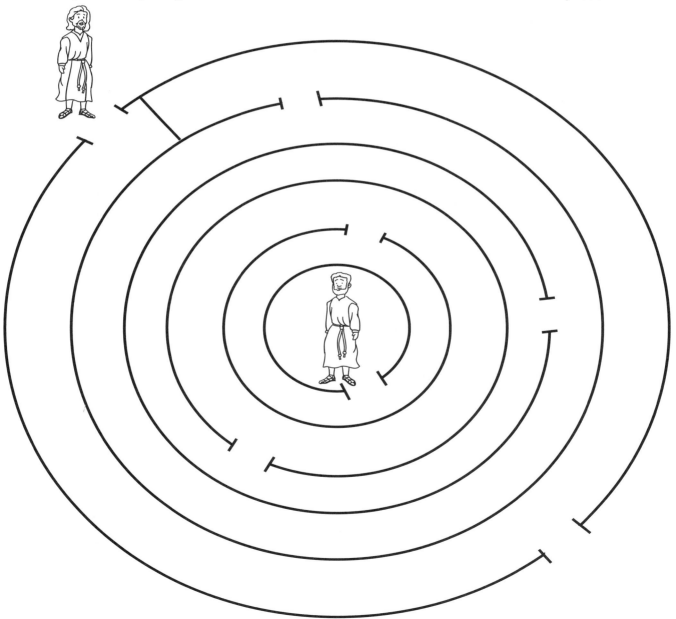

Teaching God's Word

What you need

- scissors or papercutter
- crayons or markers

What to do

1. Photocopy this page and cut out activity. Older children may be able to cut for themselves.
2. Children color pictures and number them in story order.

What to Say

These pictures tell the story of the man from Ethiopia and Philip. But they are in the wrong order! Number them in the order that the story happened. The first one is done for you.

Fridge Magnets

What you need

- card stock
- scissors
- crayons or markers

What to do

1. For each child, photocopy this page onto card stock. Cut out magnet patterns and use to trace the shape onto magnet sheets. Cut out magnets. Older children may be able to cut and trace for themselves.

2. Children color patterns and glue to matching magnet shapes.

What to Say

When you bring home your Sunday school papers, fasten them to the fridge with this magnet. Then, you can remember to tell your Bible story to your family and share God's Word.

I can share God's Word.

I can share God's Word.

Philip Teaches about Jesus

I'll Tell You about Jesus (based on Acts 8:26–39)

memory verse

Preach the Good News to everyone. Mark 16:15

discussion questions

1. What was the man Philip met reading?

2. Who did Philip teach the man about?

Sharing
God's Word

Color the picture of Philip teaching the man from Ethiopia about Jesus.

Peter Escapes Prison

memory verse

God is . . . always ready to help in times of trouble. Psalm 46:1

Go to the Temple (based on Acts 5:17–42)

After Jesus went back to heaven, Peter and some of Jesus' other friends would meet at the temple gates. It was there that they could tell others about Jesus. This made the religious leaders jealous. They had hated Jesus, and now they hated his friends.

"We don't want these people to believe in Jesus," complained one man.

"That's right," agreed another. "We need to kill these men. They will take all the people away from us."

"Guards," yelled another religious leader, "arrest those friends of Jesus, and throw them in prison."

Peter and some of Jesus' other friends were arrested and thrown into prison. God sent an angel to guide them out of prison.

"Come," the angel said. "Don't be afraid to go back to the temple and tell others about Jesus."

When they went back to the temple and started talking about Jesus again, the leaders were really angry. "Guards, go and get those men NOW!"

When Peter and the others were brought to the leaders, one of them said, "Didn't we tell you not to teach about Jesus?"

"Yes," answered Peter. "But we must obey God rather than you."

Peter knew that if he continued telling people about Jesus, he would continue to be attacked by others. But Peter also knew that no matter what happened, God would be with him, and God could help him.

discussion questions

1. Who helped Peter when he was in prison?
2. What is something you'd like God to help you with?

Story Chain

What you need

- scissors or papercutter
- crayons or markers
- glue

What to do

1. For each child and one extra, photocopy this page and cut out chain strips. Older children may be able to cut for themselves. Make a sample chain.
2. Children color strips.
3. Children loop and glue the strips together to form a chain.
4. Recite the rhyme below with children as they work.

Action Rhyme

One little man, telling about the Lord.
Hold hand out to show small height.

He was put in prison, chained to a board.
Hold hands together as if handcuffed'

Peter didn't cry and Peter didn't wail.
Rub eyes as if crying.

He waited for the angel to get him out of jail.
Flap arms as if wings.

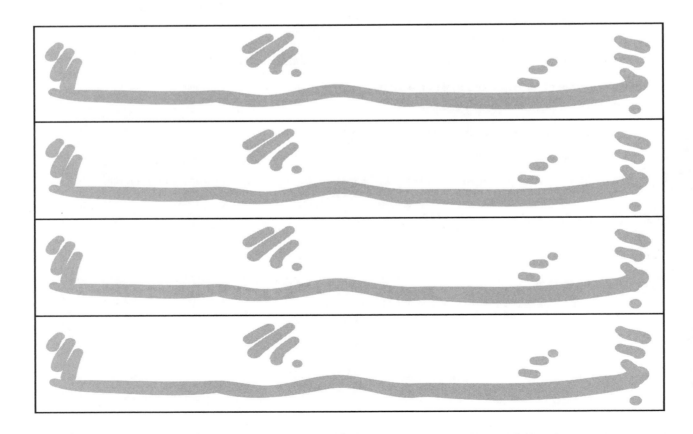

 Top 50 Creative Bible Lessons: Fun Activities for Preschoolers

What's Different?

What you need

- scissors or papercutter
- crayons or markers

What to do

1. For each child, photocopy this page and cut out activity. Older children may be able to cut for themselves.
2. Children circle the nine ways the pictures are different.
3. Children color the pictures.

What to Say

God helped Peter, and God will help you, too! No matter what's happening, you can always ask God for help.

Answers

1. window
2. smiling soldier
3. length of spear
4. Peter's hat
5. Peter's shoes
6. open door
7. chains on arm
8. angel's sash
9. angel pointing

Free from Chains

What you need

- none

What you do

1. Photocopy this page to use as reference as you teach the song and finger play to children.
2. Say the "God Took Care of Peter" and "Peter Was Freed" finger plays using the motions shown. Do each rhyme with the children a few times as they learn the motions.

God Took Care of Peter

Peter was asleep in jail.

 pretend to be asleep

There was a soldier on each side.

 touch each side of self

Then Peter heard an angel's voice

 hand to ear

And his eyes opened up wide.

open eyes wide

Peter's chains fell off his hands.

 *shake wrists*

The angel said, "Follow me."

beckon with hand

Peter was soon out of the jail.

 wave hands

His friends thanked God he was free.

praying hands

Peter Was Freed

Peter was in jail,
His hands were chained up tight.
God sent an angel
To help him in the night.

pull wrists together

Peter's chains fell off.
Angel said, "Follow me."
They walked right out of that jail.
And then Peter was free.

pull wrists apart

Peter Escapes Prison

Go to the Temple (based on Acts 5:17–42)

memory verse

God is . . . always ready to help in times of trouble. Psalm 46:1

discussion questions

1. Who helped Peter when he was in prison?

2. What is something you'd like God to help you with?

Make an Angel

God sent an angel to help Peter get out of prison. God helped Peter, and God will help you. Make an angel as a reminder that God is always ready to help you.

Cut out the angel face. You will also need a paper-towel tube and a coffee filter. Tape the angel face to the front of the towel tube, near the top. Then fold the coffee filter in half and tape it to the back of the towel tube.

finished craft

Dorcas Shows Kindness

memory verse

Be kind to each other. Ephesians 4:32

Dorcas Is Alive Again! (based on Acts 9:32–42)

In and out, in and out. Dorcas carefully pushed the needle into the fabric of the coat she was making and then pulled it out. The coat was for Levi, Naomi's little boy. Levi's father had died, and Naomi didn't have money for new clothes for her children. So Dorcas was happy she could help Naomi and Levi.

As Levi watched the fabric turn into a coat, he smiled. He liked to watch Dorcas sew.

Dorcas saw Levi's smile. "You look happy, Levi," she said.

"I am happy," Levi told her. "You are the best sewer in the world. My mommy said you are the most loving lady she knows, and I think so, too."

Dorcas smiled and said, "Sewing is what God gave me to do. I don't know how to cook well, and I'm not a very good teacher."

Levi looked at the needle in her hand. "But your needle goes right where it belongs."

"Yes, it does," agreed Dorcas.

The next afternoon, instead of Dorcas sewing in the sun, there were women, crying.

"What's wrong?" Levi asked as he pulled at his mom's dress.

"Dorcas is dead," she said to Levi, between sobs. "What are we going to do without this sweet, caring woman?"

It seemed like all the women were talking at once, telling their stories of Dorcas's generosity. Then Levi saw Peter in the crowd.

Peter walked into Dorcas's room and knelt by her body. "Get up, Dorcas," he said quietly.

Dorcas opened her eyes and sat up. When she walked out to her place in the sun, she was holding Levi's coat. The women were so happy to see her alive and well that they raised their hands and praised God. But Levi was happiest of all.

discussion questions

1. What should we say to people who are kind to us?
2. Dorcas was kind. She used the gifts God gave her to help others. What abilities do you have that you can use to show kindness to your friends or family members?

Verse Race

What you need

- card stock
- scissors
- clothesline
- spring-type clothespins
- basket
- crayons or markers
- fabric and trim scraps
- buttons
- glue

What you do

1. Photocopy and cut out a coat for each child on card stock.
2. Hang a clothesline between two chairs—low enough that the children can reach it.
3. Place the clothespins in a basket on the floor, near the middle of the clothesline.
4. Children color their coats and decorate them with fabric scraps and buttons.
5. Children form two teams and stand in two lines.
6. The first child in each line runs to the clothesline, says the memory verse to you, grabs a clothespin, and pins their robe to the line.
7. Children then run back to their lines and touch the hand of the next child in line.

Optional: If you want to have a non-competitive game, use one team. You can use a stopwatch to see how long it takes to "hang out the wash."

A Seamstress Snack

What you need

- card stock
- scissors or papercutter
- clear Con-Tact paper
- refrigerated sugar cookie dough
- baking sheet
- shoestring licorice

What you do

1. Photocopy the spools to card stock and cut them out, one for each child. Cover the spools with clear Con-Tact paper.
2. Before class, bake the cookies according to package directions. Before putting in the oven, poke two holes in each one to look like button holes. Bake the cookies.
3. After the cookies have cooled, give each child two licorice strings, a spool, and a cookie.
4. Assist each child in wrapping the licorice around the spool to look like thread, and threading a piece of licorice through the cookie button holes.

What to Say

I can show kindness to you when you are hungry by providing a snack. But what can we do to show kindness to hungry children in other countries? (Give money to organizations that feed them. Pray for them.)

"Be kind to each other."
Ephesians 4:32

A Robe from Dorcas

What you need

- colored card stock
- scissors
- hole punch
- yarn
- tape
- crayons or markers

What to do

1. For each child, photocopy this page onto card stock and cut out the robe. Older children may be able to cut for themselves.
2. Punch holes around each robe where indicated. Attach a length of yarn to one hole of each robe. Put tape over the other end of the yarn to make sewing easy.
3. Children sew the robe by putting the yarn up through one hole and down through the next.
4. Children color the robe.

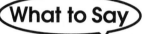

God gives each of us abilities we can use to show kindness to others. Giving hugs shows the gift of encouragement. Putting toys away neatly shows the gift of helpfulness. How will you be kind with the gifts God gave you?

Dorcas Shows Kindness

Dorcas Is Alive Again! (based on Acts 9:32–42)

memory verse

Be kind to each other. Ephesians 4:32

discussion questions

1. What should we say to people who are kind to us?

2. Dorcas was kind. She used the gifts God gave her to help others. What abilities do you have that you can use to show kindness to your friends or family members?

Caring Actions

In each row, circle the pictures that belong together. Color all the pictures.

 Top 50 Creative Bible Lessons: Fun Activities for Preschoolers

Aquila and Priscilla

memory verse

Share each other's burdens. Galatians 6:2

Helping Paul (based on Acts 18:1–4, 18–22)

Paul was a friend of Jesus'. He traveled from town to town to tell people about God's love. He wanted everyone to know that Jesus died and rose again so that we can be members of God's family.

Paul traveled all over the world! And he helped all of Jesus' followers by teaching them and writing letters. Even today, Jesus' followers are learning from Paul. We can read many of Paul's letters in the Bible.

One day, Paul was on one of his many trips. He met a man named Aquila. Aquila and his wife Priscilla were tentmakers. Paul had once been a tentmaker, too! Aquila, Priscilla, and Paul made tents to earn money to pay for their homes, clothes, and food. Making tents was their job.

Aquila and Priscilla invited Paul to live and work with them. They made him feel at home, gave him food to eat, and helped him not feel lonely. While he was with them, Paul helped them make tents. Paul was happy to make good friends like Aquila and Priscilla.

On days of worship, Paul went to the places of worship to teach people about Jesus. Eventually, it was time for Paul to go on another journey. Aquila and Priscilla went on trips with Paul to tell others about Jesus. Aquila and Priscilla were good friends to Paul and good friends to Jesus.

? discussion questions

1. What did Aquila, Priscilla, and Paul make to sell?
2. How did Aquila and Priscilla help Paul?

Stay at Our House

What you need

- scissors or papercutter
- crayons or markers

What to do

1. Photocopy this page and cut out activity. Older children may be able to cut for themselves.

2. There are four pairs of tents in the picture below. Color the three pairs that are exactly alike the same color. Color the picture of Aquila and Priscilla.

What to Say

Aquila and Priscilla helped Paul by opening their home to him. God is happy when we show his love by helping others.

 Top 50 Creative Bible Lessons: Fun Activities for Preschoolers

Tent Stories

What you need

- scissors or papercutter
- crayons or markers
- construction pape
- glue

What to do

1. For each child, photocopy this page and cut out the four scenes for each child. Older children may be able to cut for themselves.
2. Children color pictures and fold four sheets of construction paper in half to form tents.
3. Children glue one scene to one side of each paper tent.
4. As you briefly retell the story, children put the paper tents in story order.

What to Say

Tent #1 shows Paul telling others about Jesus. Tent #2 shows Aquila and Priscilla inviting Paul into their home. Tent #3 shows Aquila, Priscilla, and Paul working together. Tent #4 shows Aquila and Priscilla also teaching about Jesus.

Helping Paul Game

What you need

- scissors
- paper plate
- glue
- crayons or markers
- plastic lids, two for each child.

What to do

1. For each child, photocopy this page and cut out Aquila and Priscilla figures. Older children may be able to cut for themselves.

2. Cut one Paul figure and glue to the paper plate.

3. Children color Aquila and Priscilla figures and glue each one to a plastic lid.

4. Place Paul plate at one end of the playing area.

5. Children stand several feet away and try tossing their Aquila and Priscilla lids as close to Paul plate as possible.

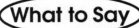

Aquila and Priscilla were friends to Paul. They showed God's love by helping Paul. They shared their home with Paul, worked with Paul, and traveled with him. We can show God's love by helping others!

Aquila and Priscilla

Helping Paul (based on Acts 18:1–4, 18–22)

memory verse

Share each other's burdens. Galatians 6:2

discussion questions

1. What did Aquila, Priscilla, and Paul make to sell?

2. How did Aquila and Priscilla help Paul?

Welcome to Our Home

Color the picture of Aquila and Priscilla welcoming Paul to their home.

Paul and Silas

memory verse

Sing to the LORD. Exodus 15:21

Singing Praises (based on Acts 16:16–34)

Paul and Silas were in trouble! They had helped a slave girl. She was sick. She could tell others what was going to happen to them in the future. The men who owned this slave girl were happy she was sick. They made lots of money by using her to tell other's fortunes.

Paul knew this wasn't pleasing to Jesus, so he asked Jesus to make her well. Once Jesus healed the slave girl, her masters couldn't make money off of her. "I can't believe that Paul!" said one of them.

"Me neither," shouted another. "Who does he think he is?"

The men were so mad that they told lies about Paul and Silas. These lies caused Paul and Silas to be arrested, beaten and thrown into prison.

Poor Paul and Silas, their hands were in stocks so they couldn't move. Their backs were burning where they had been beaten. But they weren't complaining. They weren't saying ugly things about the men who told lies about them. Instead, they were singing praises to God. Even the other prisoners could hear their praises to God and were touched by the love Paul and Silas had.

Because of the joy Paul and Silas showed, the jailer and everyone who lived in his house was saved that night. The next day, the prisoners were released. They continued to tell others about Jesus.

discussion questions

1. What does your mouth look like when you aren't happy?
2. What kind of face makes Jesus happy?

Praise Chains

What you need

- scissors or papercutter
- crayons or markers
- tape

What to do

1. Photocopy this page, making one copy for each child, plus one extra. Cut out strips. Older children may be able to cut for themselves.

2. Make a sample craft.

3. Children color strips and then tape into loops, making a chain.

What to Say

Even though Paul and Silas were in prison, they still praised God. We also can praise God, even when we have troubles.

I CAN PRAISE AT ALL TIMES

Everybody Singing Praises

What you need

- scissors or papercutter
- crayons or markers

What to do

1. Photocopy this page and cut out activity. Older children may be able to cut for themselves.

2. Children draw lines from the singing boy and girl to their smiling twins.

3. Children color the pictures.

What to Say

When you sing praises to God, your heart feels happy. When you feel happy, what does your face look like? That's right; you smile! When you finish matching the singing children with their smiling face, color in the letters at the bottom of the page. It is our memory verse. The words read "Sing to the LORD."

"Sing to the Lord."

Exodus 15:21

Joyful in Jail

What you need

- scissors or papercutter
- crayons or markers

What to do

1. For each child, photocopy this page and cut out activity. Older children may be able to cut for themselves.

2. Children color the picture, filling in the dashed lines with a black crayon.

Enrichment Idea: To make the pictures suitable for hanging, for each child, cut pieces of colored poster board 1 inch larger on all sides than the pictures. Children glue pictures to the poster board. Tape yarn loops to the back for hanging.

What to Say

There are times when we feel sad. But even though we feel sad, we can still praise God!

Paul and Silas

Singing Praises (based on Acts 16:16–34))

memory verse

Sing to the LORD. Exodus 15:21

discussion questions

1. What does your mouth look like when you aren't happy?

2. What kind of face makes Jesus happy?

Praises in Prison

There are five (5) things wrong in this picture. Can you find them? Circle them and color the picture.

Philemon and Onesimus

memory verse

If you do anything you believe is not right, you are sinning. Romans 14:23

Philemon Does the Right Thing (based on Philemon)

In Bible times, many people owned slaves. The slaves had to work in their masters' fields and homes. Some slaves were used to run errands and even were trusted to handle money for their masters.

If a slave ran away from his owner, he received severe punishment. If someone found a runaway slave, he was required to send the slave back to his master.

When Paul was in prison, he met a slave named Onesimus. The name *Onesimus* means "useful." Onesimus was the slave of one of Paul's friends, Philemon. Onesimus had run away. Paul knew he had to send him back, but Onesimus had been so kind to Paul that it made Paul sad to think Onesimus would be punished for running away.

Many people believed slaves were lazy and undisciplined. Paul wanted Philemon to know that Onesimus had been very useful, just as his name says. Paul had helped Onesimus to become a Christian. Paul wanted Philemon to know that he now could trust Onesimus because Onesimus had changed his ways.

So Paul got out his writing paper and pen, and he wrote a letter to Philemon. "Philemon, my dear friend," he wrote, "I am writing to you about Onesimus. He has been useful to me, and I would like to keep him here, but I am sending him back to you as the law requires.

"Onesimus is now a Christian brother, and I hope you accept him as one. You are trustworthy. I know you will do even more than what I ask."

Philemon was happy to welcome back Onesimus, not with punishment but with love. Paul knew Philemon could be trusted to do the right thing, and he was right.

discussion questions

1. Who did Paul trust to do the right thing?
2. How can you know if something is the right thing to do?

Bible Story Bookmark

What you need

- scissors or papercutter
- crayons or markers
- glue
- hole punch
- yarn

What to do

1. For each child, photocopy this page and cut out bookmark and pictures. Older children may be able to cut for themselves.

2. Children color the pictures.

3. Children glue the pictures in the following order on their bookmarks: Onesimus runs, Paul writes, and Philemon welcomes back Onesimus.

4. Assist in punching holes where indicated on the bookmark.

5. Cut yarn in 8-inch lengths. Tie each piece of yarn through a bookmark hole for a tassel.

6. Briefly retell the Bible story, leading children to point to the correct pictures on their bookmarks.

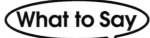

Paul did the right thing by writing to Philemon. Philemon did the right thing by welcoming Onesimus back home. God will help us know the right thing to do in everything we do.

Find the Paths

What you need

- scissors or papercutter
- red and green crayons

What to do

1. For each child, photocopy this page and cut out the maze. Older children may be able to cut for themselves.
2. Children use red crayons and find the path to Paul, starting at Onesimus.
3. Then children use green crayons to help Onesimus find the path from Paul back to Philemon.

What to Say

Onesimus was probably worried about going home to Philemon. But he knew it was the right thing to do. So with God's help, Onesimus did the right thing.

Onesimus

Paul

Philemon

What Should I Do?

What you need

- scissors or papercutter
- crayons or markers

What to do

1. For each child, photocopy this page and cut out activity. Older children may be able to cut for themselves.
2. Read the description of the first situation that is pictured. Then, read the two solutions. Discuss which is the trustworthy thing to do. Children circle the correct picture.
3. Continue with the other two situations.
4. Children color the pictures when finished.

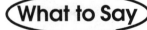

What to Say

You may not always want to do the right thing in every situation. But if you do it anyway, you'll discover that it makes you feel happy! And other people are happy, too. God is always happy when we choose to do the right thing.

Amanda promises to sweep the porch.
a) Amanda watches a video.
b) Amanda sweeps the porch.

Ryan finds a dollar.
a) Ryan puts the dollar in the offering.
b) Ryan puts the dollar in his piggy bank.

Kyle breaks Amanda's teapot.
a) Kyle tells Amanda he's sorry.
b) Kyle hides the broken pieces under his bed.

Philemon and Onesimus

Philemon Does the Right Thing (based on Philemon)

memory verse

If you do anything you believe is not right, you are sinning. Romans 14:23

discussion questions

1. Who did Paul trust to do the right thing?

2. How can you know if something is the right thing to do?

Mini Book

If you have more than one child, make enough copies of the book so that each child has one. Cut out and fold books on the dashed lines. Read the title and story to your children. Children color the pictures. Children can pair up with family members to tell the story to each other.

We like to play, but we'll do what we said.

"We will pick up our toys, Mommy."

Doing the right thing makes us happy!

Ethan and Emily Do the Right Thing

"If you do anything you believe is not right, you are sinning."
Romans 14:23

The Early Church

memory verse

They shared everything they had. Acts 4:32

Sharing Is Caring (based on Acts 4:31–37)

After Jesus went to heaven, people who believed in him continued to meet together. The Bible tells us that they boldly told others about Jesus. They loved God and each other and were excited to have others join them in following Jesus.

This group of followers came to be known as God's church—the same church, or group of believers, that we are a part of today. Since these were the very first members of God's church, we refer to them as the early church.

The people in the early church loved each other very much. They liked to share with each other. No one thought of their things as only their own. Everyone shared everything they had—their houses, their food, their clothes—everything!

The people in the early church gave money to help others. They even sold land or houses in order to have money to bring to the apostles. The apostles used the money to help anyone who needed it.

discussion questions

1. What was this first group of Jesus followers called?
2. What did some people sell so that they could give money to help the church?

Story Concentration

What you need

- scissors or papercutter
- crayons or markers

What to do

1. For each child, photocopy this page and cut out activity. Older children may be able to cut for themselves.

2. Children color pictures. Briefly retell the story as they color, indicating pictures at appropriate times.

3. Children play a game like Concentration. Children pair up and place their pictures facedown in a grid pattern.

4. Children in each pair take turns turning over two pictures, trying to find matching pictures. If the two pictures match, the player keeps the pictures. If they don't match, they are turned over again.

5. Play continues until all the cards have been matched.

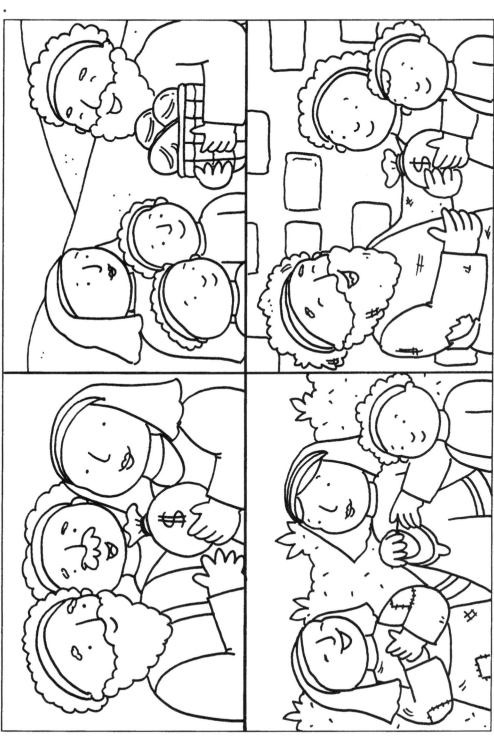

Bringing Something to Help

What you need

- scissors or papercutter
- crayons or markers

What to do

1. Photocopy this page and cut out activity. Older children may be able to cut for themselves.
2. Children use a crayon to trace the path from each of the people who have something to share to the apostiles in the middle of the page.
3. Children color the pictures.

What to Say

These people are bringing money to help others. The early church shared everything they had. The people brought many things to share with others. Some brought food, some brought clothes, others brought money. Even the children had things to share. God wants us to share what we have with others.

Sharing Wreath

What you need

- scissors or papercutter
- paper plates, one for each child
- glue
- tape
- yarn
- crayons or markers

What to do

1. For each child, photocopy this page and cut out handprints. Older children may be able to cut for themselves.

2. In the center of each plate, write the memory verse, "They shared everything they had." Acts 4:32.

3. Children arrange the handprints onto the rim of the plate and glue into place.

4. Tape a loop of yarn to the back of the plate to make a hanger.

5. Children color wreaths.

What to Say

The duck represents toys you may have. What does the hamburger represent? The shirt? The money? These are all things that you can share with others. It makes God happy when we share with others.

finished craft

The Early Church

Sharing Is Caring (based on Acts 4:31–37)

memory verse

They shared everything they had. Acts 4:32

discussion questions

1. What was this first group of Jesus followers called?

2. What did some people sell so that they could give money to help the church?

Everything They Had

Color the Bible story picture.

Top 50 Creative Bible Lessons: Fun Activities for Preschoolers